ISBN Number: 0-61529-175-9

Take It from Me: Cautionary Tales from a Former Fool

www.maynetre.com
Published by Maynetre Manuscripts, LLC

The author makes no apology for how the presence of God in this book may impact the reader's spiritual life.

Printed in the United States of America
10 9 8 7 6 5 4 3 2 1

Edited by Shantae A. Charles www.shantaecharles.com
Cover Design: ROC Studios International, Inc.

What Readers Are Saying About Take It from Me

Wedding Vows For A Marriage

"One of the best..." – Sandra Pulsifer

His Unchanging Hand

"Very strong and positive" – Andrea Charles

Seasons Change

"Just what I needed" – Tanya Footman

When Your Life Is Low

"Simply Beautiful" – Bethoria Paige

"I love it, love it, love it..." – Debbie Henderson

Take It From Me:

Cautionary Tales from a Former Fool

Tremayne Moore

Published by Maynetre Manuscripts, LLC

Acknowledgments

First and foremost, I give all thanks and praise to my Lord and Savior Jesus Christ. Thank You for salvation and the gift of Your Son. I marvel at all You've done and will continue to do in my life. You took a fool like me, and made me one of Your own.

To my immediate and extended family – I love all of you.

I want to extend my sincerest gratitude to the following individuals (who embraced the vision of this project before I saw it): Michael & Davina Stallworth; and LaShanda Callahan (and her staff at LVC Publishing) – I thank God that we crossed paths and I pray that our ministries will touch the world with His love. All that you've done for me will never be forgotten. Granted, the book concept would not have existed if it wasn't for you.

A heartfelt thanks goes to the following people: Janet (Eads) Bowling for introducing poetry to me; Brigitte Marshall for writing Andrea's prayer; Chuck & Nancy Missler (and the Koinonia House staff – also to Debbie Holland) for allowing me to use an excerpt from your magnificent book The Way of Agape (www.kingshighway.org); Howard Dayton (and the Crown Financial Ministries staff – also to Jim Armstrong) for allowing me to use an excerpt from your superb Bible Study (www.crown.org), Robert & Shantae Charles for keeping me on deadlines, for editing this book, for the great cover and photos, and for anything else I failed to mention; John & Rhesa Rudolph for answering all of my legal questions and your excellent advice; and the entire Prime Family.

I would like to extend my appreciation and love to the ministries that have impacted my life: the Lighthouse Christian Fellowship family (Drs. Ken & Deb Friendly) – Anchorage, Alaska; the Free Spirit Community Church family (the entire Kelly family) – Panama City, Florida and the Abundant Living Faith family (Dr. & Mrs. J.B. Williams) – Tallahassee, Florida. Your sermons and learning your life lessons have made such an impact in my life and it is the better after having sat under your expert tutelage.

To the young ladies at Pace Leon – thank you for keeping it real and having a listening ear during your poetry recital.

If I didn't mention your name, charge it to my head and not my heart.

Special Thanks

To my entire Four Oaks Community Church family (Pastor Erik & Tori Braun) – Tallahassee, Florida (www.fouroakschurch.com), you are the essence of Agape love. You have opened your homes and hearts to me, and I thank God for all of you. God has so much more in store for us individually and as a Church, and I look forward to basking in the blessings of God with you.

Foreword

I need to make this statement as you proceed to read this book. My dream in life was to be a singer and not a writer. I would try to write when I was nine but because what I wrote made no sense I chose not to dwell on it. A few years later, a family member was so focused on being a rapper; he encouraged me to write as he would write songs. When I look back at that period of my life (1986-1987), Hip Hop was starting to get vulgar and I tried to blend in. After a while, I stopped using vulgarity and shortly after, a classmate in high school introduced me to poetry. After writing this one poem with this classmate, I embraced the concept of poetry. I didn't know that God was going to use me to write poetry that would eventually be the making of this book. I was writing what was in my heart at that particular moment in my life while avoiding the idea of a book. After taking a long hiatus from writing, I started writing again. When I started writing again, two sisters in Christ prophetically spoke these words to me: "I have a vision. You will write something that will change someone's life, or even be quoted till the end of time." Again, I didn't think anything of it, even though numerous people encouraged me to put a book together. I was focused on writing to be a blessing to someone. Here I am, four years later, this project is no longer a vision, but a reality.

Many lives have already been blessed through the poetry God has given me to write. I pray that you open your heart to His Spirit and that you will allow Him to minister to you. Finally, I pray that you are blessed, highly favored & empowered to prosper under His hand.

For His glory:

Tremayne Moore

In Loving Memory:

My aunt Rhea Hunter

Alicia Muldrow

Makeka (Knight) Slay

You are dearly missed.

Table of Contents

Part I: Declarations....9

1. A Commitment To My Lord....10
2. A Commitment To Purity (Be Sure)....11
3. I Have a Dream....12

Part II: Food For Thought....13

1. Gabrielle's Story....14
2. If I Could (Turn The Hands Of Time)....16
3. Love and Affection....17
4. My Forgive Me List....19
5. Only A Fool....20
6. What's Wrong With Me....22

Part III: Love & Marriage....23

1. A Dream (The Wedding Poem)....24
2. A Marriage Proposal....25
3. My First And My Last Dance....26
4. My Vow (From This Day Forth)....27
5. Wedding Vows For A Marriage....29
6. When A Man Adores A Woman....31
7. When God Gave Me You....32
8. You Are Beautiful (To Me)....33

Part IV: Life Struggles....34

1. A Reflection Of Life....35
2. An Imaginary Conversation (Chapter 1)....36
3. An Imaginary Conversation (Chapter 2)....39
4. I Promise....41
5. Letting Go....42
6. The Story Of A Woman's Life (Chapters 1 & 2)....44

Part V: Tragedies....47

1. A Broken Relationship....48
2. A Cheating Story....51
3. Love's Mystery....53
4. The Story Of A Life (Parts 1-3)....55
Part VI: Redemption & Restoration....58
1. A Child's Innocence....59
2. A Single Mother's Heart....61
3. Andrea (Parts 1-3)....63
4. Starting Over....68
5. The Arms of Love....70
6. You're Still Mine....71
Part VII: Words of Wisdom....73
1. His Unchanging Hand....74
2. It's Gonna Be Alright (My Beloved Child)....75
3. Seasons Change....76
4. When Your Life Is Low....77
5. Where Is Your Dream....78
6. Who Are Your Friends....80
Part VIII: Closing Thoughts....81
1. A Place In My Heart....82
2. If I Didn't Say....83
3. Thank You....84
About The Author....86

PART I: Declarations

A Commitment to My Lord

As I look at my life, who could love me like you do?
You have given me life and I give my life back to you
There is no one who has ever loved me like you
If I ran from your presence, your love will still remain true
If I fled from your spirit, where could I go?
Your spirit is everywhere, and that's all I need to know

How could I ever repay you for all you've done for me?
If only the world and those close to me could see
The difference in me so they don't assume that I'm strange
Then they will understand that you caused my life to be rearranged
When I reached out for you, you were always there
So how could I flee from your love? I wouldn't dare

You saved my life from a lot of things
And you've hidden me under the shadow of your wings
From bad situations and bad company; Jesus, you have set me free
There's no one who changed that, no one who could ever persuade me
To go another way, no matter how they try
They are simply bad company, and their rebellion towards you makes me cry

They have actually taught me how to love the right way
And each new sunrise, I get to start a brand new day
It's because of you I can walk right
It's because of you I can talk right
I couldn't live my life without you
So, this day and going forward, I will never doubt you

When I gave my heart to you, I promised to live my life for you
So, I will forever pursue my heart to worship and adore you
I refuse to let my future be hindered by the weight of my present and past
Because I want this love I have for you to forever last
You are the author and the finisher of my faith that I will forever hold
So convict my heart when my love for you grows cold

I love you, and I mean it with all of my heart
I will perpetually praise you even if my family and friends depart
Because my life and my heart is for you and you alone
And your heart will always and forever be my home
Today, I drop my weight of problems, bad people, anger and defeat
Insanity, drama, guilt, hurts, and a heart of retreat

I refuse to play games anymore and I refuse to be bound
I lay these things at your feet because a new life is what I've found
You have given me faith and the victory to stand through it all
And I'm going all the way with you to fulfill your call
Because when my life is over, I want to hear well done
While there's breath in my nostrils, I will worship you till the day my life here is gone.

A Commitment to Purity (Be Sure)

(This poem was inspired by Karen Clark-Sheard's Be Sure).

When you love somebody? That sounds like a love song
When you've found a true love, the waiting period doesn't seem long
And the only way it's a God-sent love, it's from Him and it's pure
So as we prepare to join our hearts together, we must be sure
Yes, you're the one I prayed for, the one I waited for
We have to make it work to make this worth so much more
If it seems like I've been keeping you waiting too long
Forgive me; I want this friendship and commitment to be strong
I also want this relationship to be based on commitment and not just on love
Our commitment to God is that seal of blessing from up above
I hope I'm not pushing you away, again forgive me for my delay
In order to step to you, I need to push my emotions and thoughts out of the way
I don't want it to be infatuation, because that dies real fast
I want this to be genuine, because true love is what lasts
As we proceed to the wedding day, we must ensure
That we keep our dedication strong and allow God's Word to keep us pure
If we ever have a problem, we know that God's love is the cure
So, as we come closer to each other, we must again be sure
I do love our friendship, and I care so much about your heart
I know you've been through a lot, and I don't want to tear you apart
I want to be sensitive to your needs and love you not on my own will
Because my love would push you away with my crazy passion that kills
My love must be His love and your love must be His love
This is the foundation to our love, deep, impenetrable, unbreakable, We'll fly like beautiful doves
I remember the day we met, and yes I'll always remember
Your presence was like a cool breeze in the month of September
I want to be there for you when it's hot like June or when it's cold like December
When generations past, this legacy of love for each other they'll remember
So before I truly share my life with you
I do want to say that I don't doubt you at all, but my heart must be true
It must be right with God before I surrender my life to you
I hope you feel the same way I do
I intend to lock myself up to remain pure
So, let's nurture our friendship and make certain we're absolutely sure.

I Have a Dream

I stand today and see the dream inside of me
It's deeper than what my eyes can see
Look at me, I have ambition, I have a desire
Nobody can put water on this fire
I have this dream inside of me that's growing strong
If I can bear the short-term discomfort, the dream won't take long
I am encouraged, I am blessed, and I am a soldier in this fight
Because I'm strong in the Lord and in the power of His might
I can't let anything tie me down; I have too much at stake
I know I have to press forward and do whatever it takes.

Never to neglect the Lord who blessed me and saved me
Because it is He who loves me and it is this dream He gave me
I have to fulfill it; I have to nurture it with all of my heart
Because He knew this dream was for me from the start
I love you so much, but I have to pursue this call
Don't think that I'm pushing you away; it's not that at all
I want you to stay with me as long as you can
But I'll understand if you breeze me away like a fan
I want to please God with this dream I'm pursuing
And I don't want my life torn to pieces and turned to ruins.

I want to encourage you in your dream as I pursue mine
Because if we all pursued the dreams God gave us, the world would be fine
I'm pregnant with promise; this dream is kicking inside of me
Please understand, I have to fulfill this for us, you see
I wouldn't say this to you if I didn't love you at all
It's time we understand and fulfill what is our call
I've come too far to let my Lord down
And I must praise Him for what He's done for me in every town
If Pharaoh and Dr. King can have a dream, then I can have a dream
And when it's resurrected and affirmed, it's not as distant as it seems.

If I neglect this, I'm letting you, God, and myself down
This is my time, and I'm turning this life of mine around
Right now, I declare toxic people are going to be removed from me
They are a hindrance to me and I can't be bothered you see
I have to grow with the wheat and not live around the tares
They will be burned in the end and the thought of that, I can't bear
This is it! Destiny has to be fulfilled
I refuse to be tied down; that's not God's will
This poem might be hard for your ears, so it seems
But this is me, and I'm blessed to be living the dream.

PART II:
Food For Thought

Gabrielle's Story

(I believe the church needs a serious clean-up job if Jesus is coming back for a church without a spot or a wrinkle).

Gabrielle Thomas came to me and decided to share something that's on her heart
And from a swift assessment, I perceived something was wrong from the start
We sat at a coffee shop and she started to share with eyes full of tears
At this juncture, I'll let Gabrielle take over from here.

I've only known you for a few months, but you seem like a trusted friend
I hope this friendship we have will last till the end
I'm a little concerned about churches today and what women are looking for
Whether it's a mate, a church to please the flesh, and I believe there's more
There are three women who I love like sisters and I pray they find the right church
I also pray they test the spirits, and trust Christ to lead them in their search.

(Scene I)

Shei is 23 and she's always living in fear
Her pastor knows her well and says "She needs to be here"
Every time she goes to church, the pastor is always asking for money
That's the focus of his message, but he cloaks his purpose in like honey
If you give a specific amount of money to him, you get a special prayer
That is why the church is growing and the pastor at the church is still there
I wonder how she could sit there when he is living off the poor and middle class
He demands everyone to give an additional offering so he can travel on his yacht, what a snake in the grass.

(Scene II)

Michelle is 25 and she loves her pastor and her church
When people ask her to visit elsewhere, she says no, she's completed her search
Despite what she knows about Pastor Lawless, his down low lifestyle and his abuse of power?
She follows him blindly, talking favorably about his church and anointed choir
She knows he follows these musicians to the clubs, where big money's paid
For them to do their pernicious acts and nothing to be said

She desires a man from the congregation but is concerned that they live on the down low
She feels the pastor is anointed while his lifestyle is something no one has to know.

(Scene III)
Mecia is a single parent and she's 20 years old
She tries to model her life like a pastor's wife, covered with gold
Fancy hats, expensive clothes and jewelry, and drive a flashy car
A Lexus that is, and she feels that at this church, she can go far
The pastor degrades the women of the church and doesn't care how they feel
He will call women out specifically under the assumption he's keeping it real
Mecia is scared to leave because the pastor can easily track her down
She feels the easiest remedy is for her to skip town.

I pray for these sisters and for those who call the name of Christ
That they would open their Bible and understand that His love alone will suffice
They need to read 2 Peter 2; 1 Timothy 4; 2 Timothy 3-4 and Matthew 24
I'll leave it at those chapters, but with this topic, I could give you more
The time for playing church and living carnal ways must cease
If these people don't, they will never experience perfect peace
People must know, when you come to Christ, you surrender how you live your life
Search your heart and your church; it's time to put an end to your pain and strife.

If I Could (Turn the Hands of Time)

If I could turn back the hands of time in my lifespan
I'd see flashbacks of my life and watch the film as it ran
I'd see how I lived as my adolescent existence
And through the curious mind, temptation was a thing that required constant resistance.

Why did I fall for you, why did I let you mistreat me?
Why couldn't you let me live my life, why did this have to be?
Why did you take advantage of this innocent child?
Why did you make me feel like a child running wild?

I had to grow up fast because of my mistakes
Only to learn there were more mistakes I'd make
As my teen years blossomed, I tried to find myself
Only to learn I'm living for God and no one else.

Depression and sorrow, loneliness and despair
It seemed like no one loved me or even cared
My sin finally caught up to me
And I realize I'm in need of Thee.

Now that I found Jesus, I learn I'm still prone to sin
I'm separated from you by my sin and this new life with you I can't begin
I confess my wrongdoings to others and to you
In order to live this life and do what you want me to say and do.

Even still, I find that even after knowing you, I still fall down
But I thank you, Lord, there's forgiveness, and you can turn my life around
It's one thing to stay down, it's another thing to arise and get up
Try Him in your life; He will overfill your cup.

Even as I live my life, I find myself in conflict with sin
And my youth flashes back to me and I feel I can never win
I understand the enemy wants me to live a life of "If I Could's"
And granted, there would be some things I'd change, believe me, I would.

I can't do that, and tomorrow signals a brand new day
I need to shake off my guilt and encourage you as I encourage myself to walk in His way
We can't turn the hands of time, but we can learn from the errors of our sins
For with Jesus on our side, the fight is fixed - we win!

Love and Affection

(This poem was inspired by the Bible Study: The Way of Agape)

I know this is awkward for a poem to be about love and affection
Please stay with me because this poem has a direction
This is the day where my life gets back on track
I know I've made mistakes that I wish I could take back
Because my human frailties have hurt those I truly love
This tells me that I need to understand this agape love from above
If I told you that I love you, does that mean anything?
If I told you that I'll never try to hurt you, what joy can that bring?
When you put these questions together, you come up with a certain kind of love
It's called Storge love (a human love) and it's not from above
Hold on before you tune me out, allow me to explain
It's hard for my heart to accept this, too much for my mind to contain
Storge love is putting love and affection together
Some people think this kind of love will last forever
This love is an instinctive love like a mother to her child
It means to cover or protect, and it can become painful to the lover after awhile
Why you might ask? Well, it must be reciprocated in order for it to survive
And when it's not returned, the lover doesn't want to remain alive

Or it can turn into a possessive love, not wanting to lose that comfort zone
Of being in a married or relationship status, they're scared to be on their own
This is experienced in a dying relationship where there's a need to protect their mate
And hold on to the relationship at all costs, some of you I know can relate
It's not a love for the person that the lover is holding on to
And I'm sure that the lover cries out to God, "What wrong did I do?"
Understand that we need to let go and let God work in their lives
You can't do this alone, on your strength you'll never survive
If you don't it will be a Storge love that's suffocating and hovering
The one you love will leave anyway, because of the love that's smothering

Jealousy also plays a role in this kind of love
Some of you right now know what I'm speaking of
This is the fear of losing control of someone you love to another
And it makes you think that for you, there could never be another
This fear can motivate one's behavior or actions
And you cry when others don't meet your satisfaction
It's not an unconditional love for the person as to why you act this way
But it's a self-centered, emotional love that if unchecked, will ruin your day

The end result is then that someone becomes prey to the enemy
Due to bitterness, hate, resentment, and neither of you are free

If I've loved you this way, please forgive me
I'm trying to understand God's love so this love will be free
I know I'm not perfect, and I'm not using that as an excuse
But I'll admit, sometimes I'll throw my hands up and say, "what's the use?"
I'm never going to get this right, but that's a trap from the devil
I refuse to bow down and give in; I'm going to the next level
Back to the issue at hand, I understand this love has hurt you
I realize I need God to watch what I say and what I do
I love you too much to let you go this way
I would love to turn your cloudy moods to a sunny day
But I need God to help me do that, I can't do this alone
We need each other; it's a struggle being on my own
If I've ever appeared jealous or possessive, that wasn't my intention
I only want the best for you, and I also need to mention
That I don't ever want to be this way if we're meant to be
Because that would hurt you tremendously and in turn would hurt me
Pray for me that I learn what agape love is supposed to be
And then I can tell others about God's love is so they can see
That He's the only love that will cure this world's problems
You know and I know that He's the only one who can solve them

I hope this encourages you as it encourages me
So we can understand His love and demonstrate agape love like it's supposed to be
I must say that agape love is the only love in which Storge love can be built
I need Him and you do too, so we can experience this love to the hilt.

My Forgive Me List

Some of you may have heard me talk about this, but it's sad when immorality and drama creeps up in the body of Christ and wreaks havoc on women's hearts and spirits. But with all that said, and the things I've seen in my life, I've created a forgive me list to all of the women I've met in my life. And before you say (my single sisters), "you haven't met the right one" to me, I'd like to challenge your expectations in life. Second best shouldn't be in your vocabulary. You might find this humorous (and it should be), but it should also make you think about who's in your life that doesn't need to be.

1. Forgive me for not having a criminal record
2. Forgive me for not having an expensive car
3. Forgive me for not having gold and/or brass teeth
4. Forgive me for not calling sisters B's and W's
5. Forgive me for not being a great singer like R. Kelly
6. Forgive me for not having tattoos
7. Forgive me for not being good-looking like 50 Cent
8. Forgive me for not having a large bank account (but still have a good job)
9. Forgive me for not selling drugs
10. Forgive me for not wanting to have sex before marriage
11. Forgive me for not being a father of numerous children
12. Forgive me for not pimping you like a hot commodity.

And with all of that said what do I have to offer you?

Only a Fool

(Sometimes a blessing is right in front of us, but because we expect our blessing in a certain way, we miss it and learn the hard way. But God is still in control).

This poem will be a unique and unusual story
Either way; grab some tea and give God His glory
This story is about a woman who's special to my heart
And we both knew we were inseparable from the start
She wanted to see me face to face
And she preferred the location to be at my place
Why? She feels comforted there and knows I won't hurt her
She also knows that I'm genuine and would never desert her
Just knowing she's on her way makes my heart beat fast
The conversation she wants to discuss is about her past
I'll let her tell the story now that she's here
I hope she won't turn my joy into tears

(Woman speaks)
When I met you, I knew we were destined to be
Although the darts and temptations from the enemy I didn't see
You are the man I dreamed of having in my life
Only a fool would pass up the opportunity to be your wife
When we were together, I treated you so bad
I want to apologize to you; you're the best man I ever had
But you understand the men in my past mistreated and abused me
And much like the enemy, these men in other words used me
They only cared about themselves, not caring about my needs
Just to satisfy their egos, and their foolish greed
You were sensitive to me; you treated me like royalty
I never thought in my lifetime that a man like you would express to me your loyalty
I wasn't satisfied with how you treated me
So I said good-bye to you, and decided to be free
Free to select another man, who treated me the total opposite of you
I freely allowed these men to treat me how they wanted to
But when I saw you at the park talking to someone else
It made me ask, "What am I doing to myself?"
Only a fool would pass up somebody as special as you
I had everything I needed, a love that was so true
If I could turn back the hands of time, and do that again
I'd hold on to you, and make this last to the end
But I'm so glad you two aren't serious about each other
Because I would be devastated if you married another
I don't want to be a fool again; please forgive my behavior towards you
I want to come back to you, please believe me now; my love for you is true.

As she recites those two lines, I hold her so tight
I plan to be there for her, morning, noon and night
Of course, I accept her apology and I have to inform her of this one thing:
"I've been a fool before, but I'm so glad we're safe under His wings
With that said, let's recommit our lives to the Lord
We can fight this spiritual battle, to ensure we stay on one accord
You and I know the enemy wants to keep us apart
But if we hide His Word in our hearts, that Word in us will never depart."

Only a fool would think that love won't happen without a fight
Only a fool won't recognize the enemy wants to snuff out our lives
Only a fool would begin again without God
So my love and I give our hearts to God - really it's not so odd.

What's Wrong With Me?

When I look at my life and all of my mistakes
I wonder sometimes how much pain one man can take
I thought we as the Body were to love each other
But yet and still, I see hatred and disrespect for one another
No one wants to be honest, and we want to carry the weight on our own
I can only imagine your hurt is pain that you've never known
You want to be free, you want to run and hide
But the enemy wants you to keep the hurts and suffering inside

When somebody like me comes around
I realize that my life ends up neither lost nor found
It's scary and even saddens me when I try to be a friend
Only to find I'm kicked to the curb in the end
I thought these were people who really cared about me
Maybe I was wrong and they were hiding their true identity
I know sometimes I can be difficult, just blunt at times
But why when I try to be truthful, do you decide to drop me like a dime?
I know I won't always tickle your ear, and reality has to set in
Perhaps if I straddled the fence more, then maybe your friendship I'll win
What's wrong with me, I'd like to know how you feel
I thought people of like spirits were supposed to keep it real

Please don't criticize me and say that for you I'm too spiritual
It's a matter of trying to live right, that should be the Christian's ritual
I understand certain people can get away with things and they're forgiven
But when I make a mistake, you criticize how I'm living
I could understand it if I didn't have your best interest at heart
Then that would give you a bona fide reason to depart
What's wrong with me since I'm considered your problem?
But I know when the dust settles God can take my problems and solve them

This isn't an attack on anybody; I love you too much to hurt you this way
But we need to cast away our pride and emotions, and look for that brighter day
Nobody these days wants to be challenged in their Christian walk
So we continue to be conformed to the world and talk their way of talk
And people will continue to ridicule me for fulfilling my prophetic destiny
So, I'd like to ask those who say they believe, "what's wrong with me?"

What's wrong with me for feeling as I do?
What's wrong with me? I'm here to serve God's purposes - not you!
What's wrong with me? I've figured it out
I'm living in a different kingdom - changed from the inside out.

PART III:
Love & Marriage

A Dream (The Wedding Poem)

When I laid eyes on you, you caught me by surprise
Who would've thought you would be heavenly in my eyes?
In one glance, your complexion and your personality
It was captivating and I ask myself, is this reality?
Through busy schedules, we've survived the distance and pain
I cry at times when I look at the rain
Wanting to be with you and know you more
Then those thoughts arise that your life's not an open book but a closed door
But you proved me wrong and I've come to know you better
So consider this poem from me to you, your love letter
I see the love of Christ inside of you
And you find that pleasing Him is all I want to do
This agape love we have for Him is the perfect blend
This is not a fairy tale, nor is this some current trend
This relationship is genuine, so real that an untrained eye can't see
He created me for you, and He created you for me

As I ask for your hand in matrimony
I sit and reflect my testimony
We both had checkered pasts, but we've started anew
And there's nothing we can't conquer, nothing we can't do
As I gaze into your eyes and I take you by the hand
I see the future with you, as we walk in the sand
Footprints of our lives as our past prints are washed away
Each new step with you, marks the start of a new day
All my blessings are counted, and I give Him all His due
Because I never thought you would be to me, a dream come true.

A Marriage Proposal

(This was a conversation floating in my mind).

M:
I can't believe that we've been together this long
And I know with His love in our hearts, our bond will remain strong

W:
I know, I never had someone who would give up their life for me
But now I know that this kind of love is what Christ envisioned it to be

M:
This is such a special day, and I love you more than words can say
I wouldn't want our relationship to be any other way
Take off your shoes and unwind, I've got for you some roses and candlelight
We want to celebrate and keep it light; will sparking cider be alright?

W:
Of course, just being with you right now is on my mind
And I know each time we're together, a blessing is what I find
You care about my chastity; you care about my spiritual well-being
You challenge me to strive for perfection, and you're sensitive to my feelings

M:
All glory goes to God for allowing me to be a light to you
It's my prayer this goes on forever, in all I say and do
I can imagine God is missing an angel right now
Because He gave me to you, so at His feet I will bow

W:
I assumed relationships like this were only a dream
But you're here with me, with love flowing like a steady stream
God has truly blessed me with you, and I'm glad this dream is real
Now I need a moment to tell you how I really feel
The moment you came, you actually weren't ideal
But our lifestyles were so similar and you're the first man I could be comfortable with being real
You comforted me; you cared about my happiness
I'll admit I had my share of faults and sin; now that I will confess

M:
You're not alone; I've had my share of ups and downs
But praise God He's turned our lives around
Now here's the moment where I hold your hand and get on one knee
To ask you this simple question, "Will you marry me?"

My First and My Last Dance

As I hold your hands and we exchange our wedding vows
My heart is waiting to dance with you now
Because you know the first dance is with the one I love
You're a God-send from heaven and I've been blessed from above
You are a close second to being everything to me
I intend to protect you and love you, like it's supposed to be
Not by words or the world-kind, but like how Christ loves the church
So, you will know this love is real, and there's no need for further search
We were made for each other, and I am so blessed
We will have our blissful days, and there will be days where we feel stressed
OK, let me not wander as our vows are being said
But this is what happens when fantasies run through my head

As we leave the altar, where we accepted His call
To save us from darkness, because the cross has said it all
Our hearts are joined, and we proceed to the reception
Family and friends are there, and then there are the exceptions
But it doesn't matter, because this is your day and my day
And the devil can't hinder our joy in any way
As I take your hand, and we dance our first dance
I whisper in your ear, "I love you" like it was my last chance
I know tradition doesn't say the bride and groom also dances the last dance
But this is the story of a married life, when you look with a glance
After our first dance is over, many other dances and activities follow
Because of the strain of the day, sometimes we feel empty and hollow
But because we love each other, I know you'll save the last dance for me
I like that, saving the best for last, now that's how love should be
So because this is our wedding, flowing in our rhythm of romance
We wait till everybody leaves, and we dance the real last dance
The last dance is more touching to our hearts because this is what life is about
We start a new life with Him; however, the enemy wants to take us out
Twists and turns turn our worlds upside down
And our minds wander as if we were lost in our own town
Though I can't move as fast as that first dance we danced
I committed to this eternal romance
I know I can't move as fast as my feet
But my heart keeps the rhythm of love's timeless beat
Because Christ is first in our lives, and I know without a simple glance
That only death can separate us, because you are my first and my last dance.

My Vow (From This Day Forth)
(I dedicate this poem to my future spouse).

In a world where love grows cold and marriages are falling
Materialism is popular and no one hears the Savior's calling
Trying to be "independent" defines people of today
But we've tried it our way and failed; that's why we need His way

We need to know that independence isn't part of this Christian life
I'm talking about independence from others, even your husband or wife
We also need to know we're to be interdependent on one another
He wouldn't have it any other way; so in summary, we need each other

With that said, this is to my special someone, my future love
And I am persuaded this love will be blessed from the heavens above
From this day forth, this is my vow to you
I want to live these words in all I say and do
So baby girl, I want you to hold me accountable to this
And let these words soothe your heart and mind like a warm summer bliss
My first human counsel will be none other than you
You are my helpmate; my companion and my dream come true
I understand that most women have a sensitive and intuitive spirit
I promise to nurture that, and keep my spirit tuned to hear it
The beauty of you is that your spirit is accurate and right on time
Even if it troubles me, I won't say "I'm not paying you any mind"
I understand most men like to focus more on facts
So to maintain the proper balance, I will suppress how I normally act
The Lord truly honors your position as a helpmate to me
And I want to be a Godly man and help you fulfill your kingdom ministry
I now understand God will use you at times to speak into my life
That's why I'm so glad you've accepted this partnership as my wife
I don't ever want to bring you to a level of sub-ordinance
To where you can't speak into my life, that's not part of God's ordinance
I don't want to be apart from Him thinking you're just there when I want some
With that attitude, God's blessing to me will never come

Baby girl, the power you have is truly a blessing to me
And I pray that your light and love shines so others can see
The saying "behind every successful man is a good woman" is so true
That's why I believe that you'll ensure my gray skies are blue
I understand that I need your help in everything
And I trust that if I honor you, I'll remain under the shadow of His wing
So if I ever put you down, just know that I'm putting myself down
And the enemy would love to make me the laughing stock of the town
If I ever tell you to "shut up," know that I'm shutting up my blessing
And this forewarns me that I need to hold fast to what I'm confessing

So no matter our gifts and callings, I will seek your advice
Even when your words are rebukes or when your words are nice
When we make a wrong decision, God will be there to guide us through
Our relationship will remain intact, and our love will remain true
Neither of us should have to say to one another "I told you so"
If we ever say that to each other, we're not allowed to collect the money and pass go
When we seek each other's counsel, we're basically saying to each other, "I love you"
"I respect you; I value your insight and place no other human above you"

This is the vow to the woman who will become my wife
She is my missing rib, the one God placed in my life
In closing, I love you baby girl and you are the woman I prayed for
With the grace God has given me, you're worth waiting for
I'm empowered by you, my very own dream girl
I couldn't ask for more in this world.

Wedding Vows for a Marriage

(One day I was visualizing what a groom was saying to his bride and vice versa on their wedding day. So, I turned to Ephesians 5 and wrote the vows they said to each other. On my wedding day, I'd love for my bride to write her vows to me - smile).

(Groom)
When I look into your eyes, I know I'm truly blessed
I didn't have to search for you, and that saved me a lot of stress
You are the wife God has placed in front of me
And I trust you will be the wife God has called you to be

This is my vow to you, as I hold your hand
From this day forth, and even as we walk through the sand
I promise to love you, and be gentle with you
I will always look out for your interests in all you set out to do
I will step up to the plate and be a man after God's heart
I promise to walk in His ways to ensure nothing will tear us apart
I vow to protect you and give up my life for you if need be
I vow to ensure that in me, you will have that sense of security
I pretty much dedicate my life to you, much like how I accepted Christ into my life
And I will forever praise Him for blessing me with you as my wife
I will always take interest in your welfare in all areas of your life
I will forever say it time after time you are my heart and you're now my wife
I vow to honor you and give you the understanding that you really deserve
The one thing I don't want to do is get on your last nerve
I will appreciate everything you do, and give to you my faithfulness
For I don't want to breach your trust in me, because we have been truly blessed
I will forever love you, minute-by-minute, day-by-day
My love is your love and I will love you always

(Bride)
When I look into your eyes, I know I'm truly blessed
You found me, and sheltered me, and that saved me a lot of stress
You are the husband God has placed in front of me
And I trust you will be the husband God has called you to be

This is my vow to you, as I hold your hand
From this day forth, and even as we walk through the sand
I promise to love you, and I promise to respect you
I will submit to the leadership you are charged to do
I will step up to the plate and be a woman after God's heart
I promise to walk in His ways to ensure nothing will tear us apart
I vow to assist you and give up my life for you if need be

I vow to ensure that in me, you will have that sense of security
I pretty much dedicate my life to you, much like how I accepted Christ into my life
And I will forever praise Him for blessing me, as I become your wife
I will always take interest in your welfare in all areas of your life
I will forever say it time after time you are my heart and I'm now your wife
I vow to honor you and give you the understanding that you really deserve
The one thing I don't want to do is get on your last nerve
I will appreciate everything you do, and maintain a gentle and quiet spirit
So that still small voice from above, our spirits will be in tune to hear it
I will forever love you, minute-by-minute, day-by-day
My love is your love and I will love you always

(Both)
I will never leave you nor return to my past
I vow to you that I will work to make this marriage last
Where you go, I will go; where you rest I will rest
Your friends are my friends, and with you, I am blessed
Your God is my God, and I'm glad we serve the same Lord
You are my prayer partner, and will ensure we walk on one accord
I will forever love you, minute-by-minute, day-by-day
My love is your love and I will love you forever and for always.

When a Man Adores a Woman

When a man adores a woman, she's the only person he thinks about
He thinks about luxury places to take his woman out
He doesn't treat her like property, nor does he overstep his bounds
Because he understands he was lost before, but now he is found

When a man adores a woman, he cares about her spiritual walk
He wants to ensure they are in agreement and they talk the same talk
He wants her to mature in Christ, reaching for perfection
His hands are not to hit her, but to nurture her, giving her love and affection

When a man adores a woman, his affection isn't the world's definition
Don't worry, its Christ's kind of love, making it far from superstition
When a man adores a woman, he wants to listen to her heart
So that their love can take wings and fly straight off of the charts
When a man adores a woman, he forsakes his past friends for this love
Because he'll never turn back like Lot's wife, realizing He's blessed from above
When a man adores a woman, he dreams about her all the time
And he would contemplate ending his life if she left with no reason or rhyme
When a man adores a woman, he'll ensure her needs are constantly met
That she keeps Christ first, so that God's best they'll always get
When a man adores a woman, he will love her even if she departs
Because he knows true love never fails, he keeps that scripture close to his heart
When a man adores a woman, he would encourage her to build him up
He'd encourage her to challenge him so that he'll be filled like an overflowing cup
When a man adores a woman, he cries when she cries
His heart beats for her, so if her dreams die, his dreams die.

When a man really adores a woman, he would never abuse his position
He would ensure he doesn't wrong her, nor allow the devil to give her that premonition
When a man really adores a woman, he knows his success is tied to her success
And his life is the better because of it; he knows he's highly favored and blessed
When a man really adores a woman, he would give his life away
Not just for her, but for anyone, because he knows it's a sacrificial love we live each day
When a man really adores a woman, he will sacrifice his life if need be to prove his love
He knows that Christ died for us all, and that's real love from above.

When God Gave Me You

(I was grocery shopping one evening and a song was playing over the loudspeaker. I thought about my senior year in high school - when I thought I was in love).

When I look into your eyes, I see the beauty of His love
And I know when He gave me you; it was truly sent from above
Why did He give me somebody like you? Oh, that I'll never know
But His love for me He continually shows
But all that matters is He blessed me with you
And allow me to say this, this love we have for each other is true
There's no substitute for you, and I give my life and love to you
As Christ loved the church, I mean everything I say and do
As we walk along the shore and your hand is in mine
We talk about Christ, His love for us and our future with Him in due time
I've been many places in my life and seen so many things
I'm thankful He's numbered my hairs and kept me under His wing

As time moves forward, the enemy wants to divide us by creating walls
But nothing can come between us; I'm going to give to you my all
People around us can't tear apart what we share
You are my special love and under the love of Christ, you're my heart, and always there
If I ever give you the notion causing you to believe I'm giving up on you
Don't believe it, the enemy isn't the winner, God's Word is true

I know this is short, but I hope this is a blessing to your heart
I love you for all seasons, till death do us part.

You Are Beautiful (To Me)

(I thought about three women I met in my life; their faces and personalities inspired this poem. With that, I dedicate this to every woman reading this poem).

When I first met you, you were special to my heart
And since we know the Lord, tell me who could keep us apart?
I didn't think that I'd be able to have you as a friend
Because most people don't stay with me till the end
But you are still with me and I grow to love you every day
Although I may not show it, or maybe not in the best way
Yes, actions speak louder than words, but here's my chance
To tell you how I feel, you are beautiful even at a quick glance
Your complexion, your eyes, your gorgeous face
Every time I close my eyes, your face I can't erase
I love the feeling when I look into your eyes
I'm caught up in the rapture, now that shouldn't be a surprise
Maybe it's my mind, or maybe this is for real
But I want to be true to you, this is how I feel
You are beautiful to me, not just on the exterior
So don't ever think down on yourself, don't ever feel inferior
You know I don't ever want to upset you or make you cry
I want to protect your heart, and I will always try
You're a flower to me, and I want to keep you forever
I hope and pray we will always be together
A day not hearing from you, is the day my world ends
And I couldn't imagine living my life with this being the trend
When God took the rib from Adam, He created a masterpiece
And you are that work of art, and your beauty will never cease
I love you; I love you, what more can I say?
And it seems your beauty gets better day-by-day
You are beautiful to me, and it's my prayer that you know this
That you are exquisite and divine, your beauty no man could resist
Although it's said many times, and I mean this sincerely
You are special, a blessed woman of God and you are beautiful to me.

PART IV:
Life Struggles

Take It from Me: Cautionary Tales from a Former Fool

A Reflection of Life

(I looked at my life one day and realized it had no meaning without Christ. You could call this my Ecclesiastes).

When you look at your life, what do you see?
Do you have everything? Is your life what you want it to be?
Is God the center of your joy or is the world your hiding place?
Do you live in a fantasy with your mind and heart lost in space?

When I look at my life, I see so many things
And I'm thankful to God that I'm under the shadow of His wings
I should've been dead, expelled from school, and today be behind bars
Who would've thought He'd bring me this far?

When I look at my life, do I live this life alone?
Is there a special someone to help make my house a home?
Do I sing silly love songs? Do I wake up with no one to kiss?
Do I dream my silly dreams forever, wondering if I really exist?
Does my search for worldly happiness mean more than my salvation?
Do I seek another human to give my life validation?
Is my life focused on having someone to hold me tight?
Is my life focused on dreaming about someone? Will that help me sleep at night?
Do I say I love you and you love me in return?
Do I say I have nothing without you and not get burned?
Do I say that I'll be faithful and you run away from me?
What did I do wrong? Is this how love is supposed to be?
Can I sleep in peace without crying over you?
Is a man crying? Can he prove that his faithfulness to you is true?

Where is my life going? When does this madness end?
Do I continue on my own pursuits without searching around the bend?
Did trying to be popular in school prove who I am to others?
Only to find that no one cared about me, neither sister nor brother
Is there any existence in my life? Is there a meaning to all of this?
Maybe so, maybe not, but His trumpet call I don't want to miss

If you think I'm depressed, don't worry, everything's fine
This is just a reflection of my life, and I thank God that He is mine
For without Him, I'd continue on this search without knowing a thing
Thinking love should've came my way to carry me under its wing
It's brought nothing but pain and sorrow, and not wanting to see tomorrow
I can't be down forever, there's no time for sadness and sorrow

If we just stay in His love, nothing can go wrong
Make Him your focus to please and His Word your love song
I don't want to make you stumble, your salvation to Him is as important as mine
We have to walk this road together, and we'll make it in His time
Thank God He's brought us this far in our walk
Because we have a testimony to share each time we walk this talk.

An Imaginary Conversation (Chapter 1)

(This poem might make you think a little bit. Read it all the way through for your blessing).

(Me):
Hey my brother, can you listen to me
Something is bothering my spirit, and I know it shouldn't be
I have someone special in my life and she is everything to me
I constantly think she's a gift from God, if only she would see
We encourage each other; we keep God first in our lives
But then there are days when I need her to survive
This may sounds absurd, but I ask that you bear with me for a minute
I know my love for her will never have a limit
She loves The Lady, Her Lover, and Her Lord; and I know she's been burned before
She made it clear to me she won't take this kind of suffering anymore
She doesn't need another man in her life to bury her in the dirt
Adding another scrape to her body and another hurt
I have a suspicion that she wants to leave me
I don't know why, maybe God is trying to get me to see
That He has another plan, or maybe He's saying she is the one
She can't afford to miss her blessing; she doesn't have to be a man's bone
I don't want to save this relationship on my strength, I need Him now
Not for my will, but His; and I know He'll make a way somehow

(My Brother):
I hear you my brother, I know it can be hard at times
The Lord is saying to you, I am yours and you are mine
Don't ever neglect the still, small voice that calms your heart and mind
When you're open to Him, a blessing is what you will truly find
Now in regards to this woman who you think might be it
Stay close to Him, and don't ever get into a rage or a fit
That's what the enemy wants; for us to step outside His will
God's time is either set or appointed; He will answer and just stand still
Try a nice dinner and a dozen roses, not like a worldly man would do it
Remember she is the focus and not you, when it gets down to it
Fix her whatever she wants by candlelight
I know you can cook (that's a gift God gave you), so this can only go right
Treat her like a queen, the way God intended it to be
Erase the past from her mind, and make sure your hearts are focused on Him completely
Don't overstep your boundaries with her; she's your sister by association
Since you both know the Lord, we're separate for Him and part of a holy nation

(My Sister):
I know women struggle under the hand of the enemy

But because His blood sanctifies us, we've been set free
If my sisters could only see they can live drama free
We can get on with the things of God and fulfill our destiny
Don't rush your feelings for her, let God have His rightful place
I know there will be days that your mind will drift to outer space
The enemy wants to gain access to your thought life, don't give him a chance
He will lead you on the wrong track, if you dance the enemy's dance
If she leaves you, don't harbor bitterness in your heart
Because the Lord is in you both, you won't forever be apart
You'll see her in heaven provided you both stay on the same path
If either of you depart from the narrow way, be prepared to face His wrath
The enemy wants to keep us sisters in bondage forever
But if we're blood washed in Christ, tell the devil from this point on, never!
I don't know what this sister has been through in her past
She's probably wounded deep inside and wondering, will her exquisiteness last?
Happiness will never be found in this cold, cold world
If her spirit isn't restored, she will never be a woman; she'll remain a little girl

(Another Brother):
How good and pleasant it is when we can encourage each other like that
Sisters, arise, you don't have to be treated like a doormat
Picking up where my sister left off, I would like to see sisters challenging brothers
We are all a part of God; He created us like no other
Sisters need to help brothers, not talk them off the path of life
If you sisters treat brothers in Christ like trash, you might as well grab a knife
I'll make it plain for you; I believe you know what I'm trying to say
Brothers need to face their responsibilities like a man, and stop running away
The enemy wants to have divided Christians, and we will always face bitterness
This is why problems begat problems, and there's never any happiness
In summary, God is in control; be patient and wait
He'll never be too early, and He'll never be too late
Translation: He's on time, and you both will never be forsaken
So, if we could learn to pray and fast more, we won't be shaken

The relationship structure was designed by God to represent His love
Married couples are to represent Christ and His body, a true blessing from above
The devil is dividing families, lives, and us when you think about it

I pray you believe His word, it is powerful, and don't doubt it
We can't afford to operate on our time anymore
The enemy is looking for a crack in your heart's door
If God has truly blessed you with a mate, make sure it's from the Lord
The man is to complete a woman and vice versa, this is the meaning of one accord
God knows who to attach you to, so don't ever quench His spirit
Keep His love in your heart and His still voice; you'll always hear it
In closing: His blood cleanses our past, present and yes our future; we have the key
Allow His blood to cover you at all times, and you will truly be set free.

An Imaginary Conversation (Chapter 2)

(This poem didn't go in the direction I intended it to, so I believe that God took hold of this story).

(Me)
Hey everybody, can I talk to you for a minute
I'm glad God sent you to me; it appears my life is finished
Another struggle occurs, depression has its hold
I know God cares for me, and His plan for me will unfold
This depression is about people, and how we relate to each other
You think they'll be there for you, but if isn't one thing...it's another
My question is why do people that believe
Treat similar people like infidels, causing me to be deceived
I'm cold, lonely, and wonder if I really mean something to them
It's saddening to see church people treat me like a criminal and not the victim
People who I thought were friends turned out to be leeches
And trying to be accepted by them causes me to feel depleted.

(Single Sister)
Wait a minute! Let me stop you before I scream
First of all, God is the author of our dreams
Why are you worried about your acceptance in the world?
You're not here to please any man, woman, boy or girl
You're the righteousness of God, the apple of His eye
Walk by faith; He wants that from you and I
Those "leech people" you call friends will fall by the wayside
Don't let the enemy (who's using them) take you for a ride
It saddens me too, but I keep pressing on for His call
And I had to surrender everything to Him; yes, I do surrender all

(Single Mother)
I understand what you're saying sis, so can you hear me too?
It seems like I'm going to struggle in everything I do
I know I made mistakes, and probably will until I die
And I believe that He will forgive; He's not a man that He should lie
I love my children, and they stress me out every now and then
But I will respond to their needs whenever I can
Maybe I'm looking to the world to find my happiness
Only to find nothing, now that I will confess
I'll admit, at times my flesh takes precedence over the Lord
So I'm crying for help, I want to walk with Him on one accord

(Single Sister)
Sister girl, surrender everything you possess to Him
Your children, your body, your life; I know your light is dim
Read Matthew chapter 5 and you'll find that light

Then browse Psalm 119:11 and your light will shine bright

(Single Brother)
Amen to that, and I have to agree
So let's take this time now to cast our cares on Thee
In this world we will have tribulations
But if we are in Christ, there is therefore now no condemnation
I listened to everybody speak, now everybody stand, you're like a palm tree
So flourish through the storms and wind that will come to you and me
Don't depend on man for comfort or to fill that empty void
Now that we know the way, we must identify what we have to avoid
The enemy wants to paint a picture that sin looks good
So he can turn you upside down, and terrorize your neighborhood
Try everybody's spirit to see if it's of God, we need to be honest with ourselves
Because we individually have to give an account, it will be just you and no one else
What's saddening is the body of Christ isn't doing what it's supposed to
That's why nonbelievers don't want to come near me or you
We've allowed the world to intermingle with our spiritual beliefs
That's why we have problems, and keep asking, "How do you spell relief?"
Some of the weight held on us is of our own will
And if we could release it, we can reach the top of the Holy hill
You have to want it, and we must if we want His high call
And like my single sister said, we have to say, "Lord, I surrender all"
Let me say this one more time, you're like a palm tree
Go outside, lift your hands to the sky; your wave signifies you've been set free.

I Promise

(This poem was inspired by a conversation with a good friend of mine. Sometimes we put our people on pedestals, and that can damage a friendship and/or a relationship).

When I said I love you and I took you by the hand
We dated, we were in love, and left prints in the sand
It was a love that seemed like a once in a lifetime chance
I was yours and you were mine entangled in a divine romance
But something went wrong along the way
My smiles became tears and poured like a rainy day
You wanted to get away from me, and I tried to reason why
Searching for answers, and asking myself, "why should I even try?"
What did I do wrong, why am I putting so much pressure on me?
I'm a simple man trying to fulfill my prophetic destiny

As I sit down, realizing Jesus is my only hope
I call His name and He gives me strength to cope
It's hard, especially when's he uncovering my faults and pains
But the Word does imply that His blood is our gain
He shows me mistake after mistake that I've yet to uncover
And as He sends people to minister to me, I soon discover
That I've been living in the past with buried emotions
Will somebody say amen to that and second the notion?

Mistake number one is I've been living for love
The remedy is to forsake all and know that I'm loved from above
Mistake number two is I've placed others before me
This is in the sense of making women gods, now I see
This has been an ongoing problem and has to end
I can't live in a fantasy and I must forsake this trend
If I'm to fulfill what I'm called in this life
I have to let Him break me in order to embrace my wife
This is probably why I've pushed so many away from me
It's painful to bear, but now my blinded eyes can see
That His forgiveness is there and I have to embrace it
He's the God who can do anything including erase it
There are more mistakes that He's revealing to me
And I'm so glad about it, because now I feel so free

With that said, I'm sorry for placing you above the God of my life
I don't want to put you above God even if you're my wife
I'm sure you know that I love you, so pray my priorities get right
Pray that God will continue to break me and that my walk with Him will be tight
I know sometimes we can place each other above God
To the believer it's not right, but to the world it isn't odd
If I ever hold you again, I promise to not esteem you that high
OK, after typing that line, I need to stop and take a sigh
If you decide to come back to me, can we promise one thing?
We won't put each other on a pedestal, and we will stay under His wing
Stay tuned to His spirit and I promise to do the same
Because I pray that we will be ready when He calls our names.

Letting Go

(Letting go is hard especially if you care for someone and they decide to leave. Sometimes we forget that God may be saying to us that their purpose in our life is completed).

I guess the hardest thing in life is to let someone go
But I can't control your heart, only you know and only God knows
I can't make you love me; I can't make you stay with me forever
Because time and seasons change, so you can't say you'll leave me never
Tomorrow is never promised, and flowers die every day
I know this situation is sad, but we have to face it any way
As you walk out of my life, I try to hide my tears
I can't pretend, so I have to surrender to God all of my fears
Because if I don't, I'll be wearing a Christian mask
And I can't live that kind of lie, nor complete my daily tasks
I guess letting go must be done with our hearts
And giving it all to Christ so that He can take us far
Farther than our hearts can dream, beyond what we all can see
But let's bring it back home for a minute; let's talk about you and me
Even if I said I love you, what does it mean to you?
If I said that I'll try to never hurt you, what would you do?
Notice I didn't say that I'm letting go of you
Because I love you with the love of Christ, that's the only thing I can do
If you really want to leave my life, then maybe I have to let you go
But if you want to come back, I'll never say no
You are special to me, and you share a place in my heart
I remember saying to you that nothing could tear us apart
And if we know the Lord, nothing can come between us two
I mean that with all of my heart, and no matter what you may do
I'll always be there for you because it's not about me anymore
I care about you and your heart, and I'm willing to lay it down like never before

As I watch you walk away and leave my life and my heart
I try hard not to cry, it seems like I've been forsaken because you decided to depart
There's nothing I can do to stop you, nothing I could say
Your mind's made up and I now have to face a new day
A new day without you makes it hard to cope
But good things and blessings for you is what I hope
I pray God's Love will shower your mind, spirit and heart
Because He's the one who taught us about letting go from the start
He gave up His life so we could gain forever
And I know this may sound strange to some, but He won't leave us, no, never
So in turn, He wants us to let go of our lives and lay them down
So we can obtain the heavenly prize and cast our golden crowns

I know this poem took a deep turn, but stay with me please
How many of you agree that we all need to be on our knees
And cry out to Him for His Love to rain down on us
Because His standards are right, and His ways are just
So, when our lives are over, He'll be able to take us home
Are you ready to go? Because the best is truly yet to come
Stand with me; agree with me, this race is almost won
Hold on, stay on track, we can make it with the Son
So, even if you depart from me and if we stay with His Love
I love you, and I'll see you again, as we will fly together like doves.

The Story of a Woman's Life (Chapters 1 & 2)
(I thought about all of the women I've met in my life and decided to summarize my experiences with them in this story).

(Chapter 1)

As I walk outside, what do I see?
A beautiful woman as she steadily approaches me
She has been abused, and she's also a mother
And men have taken advantage of her like no other
As she pours her heart to me, what do I learn?
I learn that her respect is what I've got to earn
She's lost her confidence, she's lost her poise
And she's really tired of hearing a man's noise
She knows I'm a Christian and perceives I'm trying to live right
So we talk on the phone day after day, and night after night
She also knows I'm genuine and real with my beliefs
There are times she's thinking like Charlie Brown, "good grief"
She tells me that she believes, but her man doesn't want to hear that
Maybe I can try to change him, but he hits you with a baseball bat
It's the same situation that she's been in before
It's the same stronghold that's knocking at her door
As I try to be an example, she pushes me away
Don't fall in love with me, because I just lost my man today
He just got involved with somebody else
And left me to raise my child all by myself
I ask her does she like being bound by the devil
When she can really live her life at the next level
But she constantly tells me you're not my type
You're too good for me, even though you don't have hype
You deserve somebody better, so she continues living her days
Wondering if the men in her life will ever change their ways
I really want to ask her, where is your self-worth?
You have something to offer (other than your body) to this earth
Why can you see I'm trying to be a witness and a light?
You don't have to hold your pillow when you cry at night
There's a light at the end of the tunnel, will you believe me
If you forsake this world, trust me, a better life you'll see
The world won't miss you when you forsake its gold
Take Christ at His word, that's what you need to hold
Don't pass up a brother who's really trying to please God
Just because he doesn't meet "your" standards, doesn't mean he's not from God
He should be "your" standard, if His standards are in your heart
So arise, my beautiful sister, He's your friend that will never depart
I thank you for allowing me to be a blessing to your life
Save yourself, to be that strong Godly wife!

Take It from Me: Cautionary Tales from a Former Fool

(Chapter 2)

The second chapter begins as she continues to live her life
She's trying so desperately to become somebody's wife
Maybe her man believes, maybe he doesn't care about Christ
He looks good to her and has cash, I guess for her that will suffice
She loves reading literature about drama in our world
And the drama affects this once innocent girl
She lives her life with caution, burdened by her past
And she probably looks in the mirror, wondering will her attractiveness last
She lost her worth that was in Christ for the world's desires
Or maybe she combined the two, either way, that's playing with fire
She lets circumstances and her man define who she is to the world
And she will believe what he says, even if she's not that kind of girl
She steadily falls in and out of love, hoping she will find a man
To provide for her children in the best way he can
But maybe she doesn't have children but desires the comfort of a man
Maybe that's the plan for her life, or maybe that's not God's ultimate plan
For some women, men who say they believe are nothing but strongholds
If you cast them down and leave them in the cold
Either they'll straighten up or remain trifling, but don't wait for that pathetic man
That's what he is if he doesn't fulfill in his life God's plan
But as she continues to live her life in this mean old world
The enemy plagues her making it difficult to be God's girl
He wants her to be strong and repellant to anyone who would try to approach
And believe me, she will stomp any man as if they were a cockroach
Once upon a time she read the Bible, now she's caught in the trap of life
The drama, the abuse, and her heart endures a war of pain and strife
So when she sees me, she finds the strength to say I'm not the one
You're the problem, you don't know who you are, but problems I have none
She's buried her problems with the anger of her past
She won't lay them down so she could be free at last
Surrender is hard, even though it's easier said than done
But it requires faith when you seek help from the Great One
Nothing is too hard for Him to handle
You're a blessing to men like me; you have a beautiful light like a candle
Don't repel me because I don't agree with everything you believe
I'm not a heretic, but trust God and you will receive
A greater blessing, and who knows, you might be called to a single life
Or maybe you are called to be that special Godly wife
Hold on, everything's going to be all right
And you can make it; it's really close in sight
Repel the drama that the world is feeding you

It's tempting like forbidden fruit, but it's making you feel like it needs you
To go with it's plan and that you can find your strength without Christ
Or a power within New Age mysticism, but Christ alone will suffice
He will never let you down, and if you turn to Him, He'll erase your past
And you will have a glow and an attractiveness that will always last
Seek His face, and His advice, and His goal that we should continually strive
If we both believe in the same Christ who rose, we need each other to survive.

PART V:
Tragedies

A Broken Relationship

(This poem addresses domestic abuse. I believe if a man hits a woman, he doesn't deserve her).

This is the story of Marvin and Heather
They were so happy in love and always together
Two childhood friends that would blossom and become serious
And to think they weren't dating would truly be delirious
They went to the same church; but Marvin's choice would prevail
Heather wasn't too thrilled about it, because the pastor was always on her tail
Marvin liked it because of how the men there behaved
They were to have total control over their women, making them domestic slaves

One day, I'd meet Heather as she walked into my bank
And to see someone as beautiful as her, made my heart tank
Her spirit was troubled, so she poured her heart out to me
I would grow to love her as we talked periodically
Our friendship truly blossomed and I really wanted to take her out
But when she called saying she needed to see me now, I'm thinking, what's this about?
So I immediately went to her rescue, caring less if the police were following me
She had two black eyes and what she revealed to me was plain to see
He followed their pastor's teachings, and he beat her, trying to reshape her reality
He'd always been this way, but she thought she could change his personality
The problem remained that he's abused her before
And she tried to build up the strength to say that she's not taking this anymore
I hold her in my arms so delicately on the couch caressing her lovely face
I was so determined because of how I was holding her, not to leave her place
I think back to when I met Heather; she had a beautiful mouth and smile
But I saw such a beauty in her that I would think about her for a long while
Anyway, I comforted her by saying you need a man that will love and serve You
If he has to hit you, baby, with all sincerity, he doesn't deserve you
Just so you know, when I first met you, I thought you were beautiful to me
You still are, and I wonder if you look in the mirror, if this is what you see
A beautiful sister who God loves so very much
That if you would love Him, He'll take your life and heal you with His touch

I hope you don't take offense to me saying this, but being honest is all I can do
Heather, because I see a bond between us, I want to say that I love you
She said it's OK, and she had something to say
She said she treasures our friendship and she wouldn't have it any other way
She's quitting her job because Marvin knows where she works and because of job stress
She feels with her new job, he doesn't know where she is and now she feels blessed

A couple of days pass, and I try to call her on the cell phone
After the first or second ring, it went to voicemail and I'm feeling so alone
I sense she's ignoring me and maybe she's trying to say something to me
So I decide to let some weeks pass thinking maybe she wants me to let her be
So I decide to go by her new job, and bring her this bouquet of flowers
Praying she leaves him and the church, because the pastor doesn't acknowledge God's power
He's a control freak and the women don't deserve to be treated that way
Because their man stays there, they pray to make it through another day

The receptionist says to me she doesn't even work there
I'm thinking why did she lie to me, but I'd opted not to accuse her, I wouldn't dare
I drive over to her prior job, and as I walk inside, I see Marvin and Heather
They're talking and it appears she forgave him and they're back together
She sees me but avoids me, so I remove myself with my flowers from the scene
So, I sit in my car crying, wondering why Heather's falling for the devil's scheme
She must have taken offense to me saying I love her and she didn't need him
Why? I wondered, but God's love wants to overfill her cup, not just to the brim
They both walk outside and they cross the street, he then starts his rampage
You would think Marvin was a lion trapped inside of a cage
He hits Heather so hard that the back of her head hits the gravel
And because the impact was so hard, her hitting the ground wasn't a long travel
I immediately called 911 on my cell phone and the police arrive at the scene
I'm thinking now Marvin can be free from the devil's scheme
But sadly, I was wrong, the police let him go, but Heather's life was looking dim

She ends up in a coma, and I pray that Marvin would truly give his life to Him.
He doesn't go by the hospital to see her, but I'm continuously praying for her life
Whether it's at home or by her bedside, and that if it's His will, she will be my wife
Provided she makes it out of the coma of course, but more importantly, she knows Him
But what I said before remains valid, Heather's life is looking dim
While I was praying by her bedside and her family was also at her bedside with me
She comes out for a moment, and asks God for forgiveness and for her spirit to be free
God answered her prayer and her spirit is now free
Now I know that I'll see her again when my work here is done and He takes me.

Take It from Me: Cautionary Tales from a Former Fool

A Cheating Story

I met a beautiful angel at church one day
I never thought someone that attractive would walk my way
As we stared into each other's eyes, it was love at first sight
And knowing she was the one for me was my thought that night
As next Sunday arrived we sat beside each other
It's a fascinating thought and I think there'll never be another
To see us worshiping the Lord with lifted hands
I imagine what life would be like walking with her barefooted in the sand.

A few months later, we start dating each other
We promised to be honest with each other, never to hurt one another
But one night, as I'm hugging her good-night
She gets a phone call from her girlfriends and she's gone - faster than the speed of light
She leaves me abandoned to go out with her friends
She calls me the next morning telling me where she's been
She said, I went out with the girls and that's all she says to me
But little did she know, I kept a journal and noted, "How can this be?"
I know deep down inside that she's with another man
I'm not going to accuse her yet, but hold on to the hope that I'm her dream man
Maybe I'm just a fool in love, but I honestly love this girl
If only she knew how much she meant to me in this world.

This trend would go on for a good period of time
But I'm holding on to the belief that I'm hers and she's mine
She tells me over and over again there's no one else in her life
And that with me, she feels secure enough to be my help meet, my wife
What she said goes into my journal as well
But I knew something was wrong, at this point, it's easy to tell
No one had to tell me, I just knew it deep down inside
And the tears I cry, apart from her of course, I can't hide
I sit and wonder, to prove my love for her, what do I have to do?
I asked her that, and she said you have nothing to prove, and I love you too.

One day, she tells me that she now works at a different place
And I think, "When can I surprise her at her job with my face?"
I go to the jewelry store and purchase an engagement ring
And buy a dozen of roses in a vase, yeah, that's what I'll bring
I go by her job, only to find that she doesn't work there
So, now I begin to wonder, confusion's got me running scared
I drive to her prior job, and the receptionist buzzes her down
I'm so jumpy at this point, am I acting like a clown?
She comes off the elevator and she's accompanied with a man

Take It from Me: Cautionary Tales from a Former Fool

I try to keep my composure the best that I can
She says to me, this is the man I've been with all this time
And I thought back to when I believed that I'm hers and she's mine
I drop the ring onto the floor and the vase crashes to the ground
I thought I was her king, apparently I'm the clown.
I run out the door in tears, and she runs after me out the door
He stands there encouraging her, "you don't have to answer him anymore!"
He has no remorse for what he's done, and wouldn't you know
She didn't have the wisdom to realize she was the fool to let me go
She's also two months pregnant and he met her through her friends
He curses God in front of her, but somehow, I thought this was the end.

As I'm running away from the scene, feeling my life has no rhythm or rhyme
She catches me outside and I told her I knew it all this time
She said, if no one told you, you would've never known
And I told her point blank, that Satan's cover would eventually be blown
If you were to look through my journal, you'll find my inner thoughts there
I knew you were cheating and I was hoping you would tell me you didn't care
Instead of leading me on believing you really loved me
What more can I say? I have to let you be

I jump into the car and make it only two blocks
A gray Ford Mustang sideswipes my car and I'm dead at 2 o'clock
She on the other hand, endures emotional abuse from this man
She tries to hold on to the relationship the best that she can
One night, he comes home drunk and starts the abuse
This time, she throws up her hands and says "what's the use?
I'm stuck with this man and I'm going to die with this man
I'll stick it out with him the best that I can."
Well, she did, while drunk he killed her and the unborn child
And the sad part about it is that he's out of jail after a while
That while is only two months, and he's now back on the streets
Looking for some innocent girl that's so naïve to beat
My pastor found out the news about our deaths and he cried
He told his church, "The world needs to know that justice delayed is justice denied!"

Once upon a time, I fell in love with a girl
And I naively believed she was everything I needed in this world
I didn't think a girl this special would be so easy to find
But looking at it now, she wasn't a beautiful angel, I was just blind.

Love's Mystery

(This poem is to encourage us to not let love dictate the terms of our existence. If anything let God's love dictate the terms of our existence. Once we do this, we'll understand the mystery of love).

Have you ever met someone and your heart beats fast?
And you think the friendship with that someone will last?
Some stand through the test of time, and some don't stand a chance
But you'd like to one day be with that someone for the first dance?

When I met you, I didn't know what to think
But your smile sent a chill through me and made my heart sink
It's a beautiful thing, believe me it's true
But sometimes I feel like I have nothing if I don't have you
Has love taken a toll on me, acting like a child with a new toy?
Who would've thought that love could give a person so much joy?
I'm sure somebody can relate to this, if so, can you say amen?
But when love lets you down, you think "what a fool I've been"
Isn't love a mystery even when you know God is in control?
Maybe it's our flesh taking over our mind, body and soul?

Continuing with the story, the friendship is growing
It's lovely as a cherry blossom, that's what our eyes our showing
It goes on for days and I dream of spending my life with you
And I dream of the day to hear that you feel the same way too
As I pour out my heart, love comes knocking at my door
It takes the one I love away, and I've seen this many times before
"I should be used to this" you would think and probably would say to me
Have you seen this before? If only your eyes could see
Love has pulled my heart out from me and what do I find?
It's shattered like broken glass, and seeing it crushes my mind
I think of her constantly and minutes turn to hours then to days
And I pray for the day you will again pass my way
Rumor has it, you are actually leaving town today
I don't know what to think and I really don't know what to say
Isn't love a mystery even when you know God is in control?
Maybe it's our flesh taking over our mind, body and soul?

I spend many weekends walking along beaches and shores
Saying to myself, "I can't go on like this anymore"
"I feel like my destiny is to be single, a life with no one to share"
"Even though I'm what women dream of, if only they would dare"
But then, out of the blue my cell phone rings
After three months you call, and my heart wants to sing
The excitement is short-lived, you're married; he took you away
I jump into the ocean thinking to myself, "what more can I say?"
My cell phone no longer works; my heart rate has decreased

Take It from Me: Cautionary Tales from a Former Fool
The water covers my face, and after ten minutes, I am deceased

In the midst of this fictional tale, there is a moral to this story
And it's my heart's desire that God gets all of the glory
Many of us have been hurt by love before
And because of this, you've shut to other people your heart's door
Today is a new day; release yourself from your past
You have a splendor given to you by God, stay in Him and it will last
Let your past go, because if you don't you will never be set free
The devil has a hold on you, binding you to who you're called to be
Don't just jump into a relationship to cover your past sins, hurts, and pains
You'll just complicate matters in the name of love with nothing to gain
Don't trust your heart, the prophet said, "Who can know it?"
Proverbs says to guard it, because what's inside of it, you'll show it
It's time to be honest with God and most of all with yourself
We have to trust God with everything (even love) and no one else
Give Him your hurts, and give your past one last cry
His love will heal your emotional wounds and holes, please give Him a try
When you can look God and yourself in the eye for real
And say, "I can do all things through Him" despite how you feel
That's your first step to freedom; now walk in that liberty
And as you walk with Him, you'll be able to understand love's true mystery.

The Story of a Life (Parts 1 - 3)

(I always wanted to write a poem focusing on my eulogy. This poem also addresses financial and marital infidelity. The moral is that God showed up in the end).

Once upon a time, I, a mere man, fell in love
(Part 1)
I believed she's an angel sent from above
We get to know each other, we date, and people can see
That we were made for each other, destined to be
We attend the same church, worshiping the Lord together
We encourage each other to love Christ forever
As the days progress, my love for her truly grows
And the more I'm around you, the more I know
I tell her: I want to spend the rest of my life with you
So, we exchange vows as we say to each other "I do"
I always knew that you would make a beautiful bride
And honey, we can't lose with Christ on our side
As we leave the church, my life with her begins
And I constantly pray that this happiness will never end

It's Friday morning, and you're watching the sunrise
I come to you from behind and you're not even surprised
I place my hands around your waist and you place your hands on mine
Do we have to go to work? Must we be constrained by time?
So we go to work, but you called me early afternoon
Right in the middle of my favorite Bugs Bunny cartoon
Out of the blue, you say, "I'm not coming home tonight
This love I have for you now doesn't seem right
So I'm going to stay with a male friend to get away from you
Why am I starting to hate you? Why do I feel the way I do?"

I hang up the phone wondering what created this feud.

(Part 2)
A couple of weeks pass, and I come home from work confused
Wondering if she's having an affair, or if she's being abused
I constantly pray for her, and as I place the key in my door
Somebody tells me that you've dropped by a couple of times before
I walk to the bedroom and find another man's clothes on the bedroom floor
So, I leave the bedroom and close the bedroom door
I go to check the mail, and find my credit card bill
I see the amount, and I try so hard to stand still
She maxed out our credit card and I immediately drop to my knees
I've faced two situations and I need to be spiritually free

The Lord in His still small voice reminds me that everything is going to be fine
I read Hosea, Matthew 24:12 and Matthew 11:29

After reading the passages, I decide to go to the park
It's better to do it now before it gets too dark
I'm no longer mad at her; He removed the hurt feelings from my broken heart and mind
I confessed those sins to God and start praying for her safety and for her to find
That first love when she accepted Christ for the first time
Praying that she remembers that I am hers and she is mine
I jump in my car; celebrating the freedom God has given me
I'm sitting at a red light, feeling so free
As the light turns green, and barely making it out of the intersection
A green Ford Mustang running a red light, comes to my direction
It hits me, and all of the cars slow down and look but they just pass
Because it hit my door, my face is covered with blood from the impact and broken glass
The driver didn't have insurance; the police, without citation, let him go
But he was the one that ran the red light, well, what do you know?

At this point, I'm unconscious, and my world seems deluded.

(Part 3)
I wake up hours later, in a hospital bed
I have two punctured ribs, that's what the doctor said
They wondered how I made it out of the accident alive
I say to them, it's God's grace that gives me the strength to survive
I'm to be in the hospital for about a year
The next thing the doctor says makes me burst into tears
I didn't know this but they found a tumor in my brain
And the stress pressure is causing a horrible strain
As my chances to live get slimmer by the day
No one visits me, everyone's abandoned me, and I start to pray
As I sing "all to thee my blessed savior, I surrender all"
I close my eyes, and I hear the angel of the Lord call

(Epilogue)
This was what I wrote as a speaker at my own funeral, the pastor said
He wrote this speech two days before his death on his hospital bed

Growing up wasn't easy, I had some demons to face in my life
I had to endure abuse and a lot of unnecessary strife
I had people who in their own interest, took advantage of me
But I didn't let that stop me from fulfilling my destiny
I always wanted to make you happy and help you fulfill your calling

I wanted to be a brother for you, and keep you from falling
Now that I'm gone, how will you continue to live your life?
Are you going to pick up your Bible and learn to be a faithful husband or wife?
Are you going to turn your life around, and make this your lifeline?
Are you going to choose life and turn from your wicked ways this time?
Tomorrow's never promised, as you can see, I'm not hear today
I know you really didn't care about me because you turned the other way
When I tried to be a friend, you didn't want to hear me
When I tried to be a man, you thought I wasn't man of integrity
But how do you feel now that I have departed from you?
Will you continue to live the way you do?
I pray that God's love and mercy will reign in your hearts
And nothing will tear your love for Him apart.

There was more to that speech that the pastor read to the congregation
He could tell that people were reluctant to come to this occasion
So, when the pastor preached his lesson about the cross and His love for His bride
You can tell that the people in the pews one by one were swallowing their pride
My wife, who was there, cried and ask God to forgive her for her wrongs
She stood up from where she was sitting and sang this song:
"I surrender all, I surrender all"
"All to thee, my blessed Savior, I surrender all"

Everybody at the church came to the front during the altar call
Everybody was in tears, they've experienced firsthand there's room at the cross for all

This was my prayer that through my death, Christ would be glorified
If a soul was reached through this, then I'm satisfied.

PART VI:
Redemption & Restoration

A Child's Innocence

Once upon a time, there was a little girl
She was her parents pride and joy, and probably their world
The innocence of this girl began to drift away
As she's living in this sin-fested world each and every day
Through no fault of her own, the devil takes her captive
And the next thing you realize, the girl is sexually active
The pain lingers within the child as she sleeps at night
What did I do wrong? Can I ever do anything right?
The teen years seem so strange to this girl
What does life have to offer her in this crazy mixed up world?
Through boyfriends and lady friends, cheerleading and church
Trying to find the right love, that's the woman's primary search
But only to find the devil showing up again in her world
It seems like dark days are seen through the eyes of this girl
Through adulthood, the suffering is kept inside
And a smile is displayed to the world to cover the tears she hides.

Another girl was loved and protected by God
Don't worry, this isn't strange and it surely isn't odd
She faced adolescence with no worries and fear
She always kept the love of her family and friends near
Through the teen years (and maybe adulthood), life comes to a dead stop
And the devil has spun her life around like a musical top
What happened? The darkness closes her world
And this pain has really tortured this once innocent girl
The love she once found truly stabbed her in the back
But it was the devil's love, my correction; his love is really an attack
She thought she had found an everlasting love
But it was a counterfeit love, not manufactured from above
Through a demonic spirit, life becomes harder to progress
And it looks like the devil tore to pieces her beautiful dress.

A jewel (and some received more) was given to you from above
Even through the heartache and pain, He still gives to you His love
The father of your jewel can't or won't step up to the plate
But if you dedicate your jewel and return to Him, He'll clean your slate
He will be your husband and father to your precious pearl
He loves you truly more than this crazy mixed up world
Don't ever compromise Godly standards for anybody in this life
Because you might forfeit becoming that Godly wife.

If I could cry your tears, they would pour like rain
For everything you've been through, your hurts and your pains
To my beloved sister, you are special and you are loved
You have found a love truly sent from up above

It's my prayer that you go from glory to glory
Then you'll be able to truly sing, "This is my story."
You've been given a tremendous testimony
So dedicate that testimony and your life to Him only
Take your candle and let it burn through the night
For you are an inspiration to those who can't see the light
I treasure you my sister, for like you there's no other
Because if it weren't for you sisters, there would be no brothers.

A Single Mother's Heart

(This is dedicated to the single mothers).

Through marriage, sin, or an unforeseen midnight
A newborn baby enters the world and sees the light
The people who really love you give you their heart
But the ones you thought would be there, they would simply depart
Leaving you to carry the weight by yourself
And thoughts of hurt and guilt affect you and no one else
As life changes before your eyes, and your baby grows
Your child starts to try you like you would never know
You never thought motherhood would be like this
But nothing touches your heart than when your child gives you a kiss
The burden of motherhood takes a toll on your life
And it feels like your brain becomes used to the pain of a knife
Headaches, stress, the father not being a man
And you're trying to keep your sanity as long as you can.

I know it feels like you're in this battle alone
Understand the Lord wants you to make His heart your home
I know sometimes you don't want to be a parent, let alone a mother
But the Lord gave you a gift and loves you like no other
Continue to trust Him even through your mistakes
Because there's refuge in Him and unlike man, He won't bend or break
Don't try to carry the load you're carrying by yourself
It will bring anxiety and pain, and you'll get hurt if nothing else
Realize that if you know the Lord, you've experienced the new birth
So know that your help is from Him who made heaven and earth
He wants you to come to Him when you're weary
He'll wipe your tears when you cry at night and rescue you when you're dreary
Take His yoke and find rest in your soul and heart
Don't grow weary, and His love for you will never depart
Rise up from your pity party, and turn to the author of your faith
He said I'll never leave or forsake you, as you patiently wait
The devil wants you to stay depressed, and hopelessly down
And then you end up calling your depressed friend across town
Little did you know, that friend made your problem grow
Now you're really stressed out and God's will is crowded out by what you think you know
Don't compromise your Godly standards that He placed inside of you
Because He loves you more than what you do.

Wait on Him and everything's going to be alright
Because God can be your husband and will be your shoulder when you cry at night
Indeed, He is on time, know that He's just a prayer away

Don't neglect Him, because you can't survive without Him in your life every day.
When you're done caring, cradling, and nurturing all the while
Don't forget to let God hold you in His arms; drop the weight of motherhood, and just find rest as His child.

Here are some passages for you whenever you feel like life has dished you a bad blow, you feel like you're in this battle alone, or you feel that God is far away from you:

1. Matthew 11:28-30
2. Psalm 121
3. Galatians 6:9
4. Hebrews 4:16
5. Philippians 4:11-13

Take It from Me: Cautionary Tales from a Former Fool

Andrea (Parts 1 - 3)

Andrea's prayer: written by Brigitte Marshall
(This poem addresses HIV/AIDS awareness)

(Part 1)
I decided to go to the club on a Friday night
The men were looking smooth and the ladies were looking tight
I managed to find a table where I could sit by myself
Where I could just chill and watch everyone else
Act crazy, or just dance as if they were in a competition
Out of the blue, someone walked up, and I said, this can't be superstition
A short woman, with a short hair cut and light brown eyes
Asked if she could join me, I said of course and I would soon realize
That this is no ordinary woman who's sitting across from me
I thought to myself, "Wow, I'm 25 and she's 23"
The DJ said, "Let's slow this party down," and he played Kirk Franklin's Lean on Me
We danced to this song and I wondered could this really be?
She told me her name and I thought it suited her well
It's Andrea Cynthia Gardner and I thought she could tell
That I started to like her and I sensed that she liked me too
I thought, "Now I've been passed up for thugs, is this really true?"

We decided to rendezvous at a café on a Saturday afternoon
We mellowed out as we listened to a jazz tune
She told me she's been through storms in her life
And she wondered if she would one day be somebody's wife
She dated a man who lived on the down low and smoked weed behind her back
He was shooting needles and she didn't know if he was also smoking crack
She wouldn't find out the truth until he tried to get her involved
She ended the relationship immediately; that was the first problem solved
The second problem was she miscarried after 4 months into her pregnancy
After her miscarriage, she took time to decide what she wanted her life to be
I listened intently thinking, "Wow, her life was as rough as mine"
I said, "This is my story, if you will allow me to have a moment of your time
A trusted family member physically and sexually abused me at ten
And I lost my virginity at eleven; I didn't know the truth back then
It took me till I was eighteen to understand what real love is
I know I need to get saved; maybe this is why we're talking about this."
We poured out our hearts to each other as we dined
I realized I wanted to be hers and hoped she wanted to be mine.

(Part 2)
After a few months of conversing, we began to date

She was diagnosed with HIV, and the devil tried to damage her heart by sowing seeds of hate
But the devil lost that battle, and I proposed to her one night
And when she saw the engagement ring, she said yes and held me so tight
I decided to go to church the next Sunday; she was reluctant to come that day
I went up to the altar and got saved, but she felt she could serve God her own way
We still carried on, preparing for the most important day of our lives
That I would be her husband and she would be my wife
The wedding was captivating as we were married in Disney World
To see her come out of the pumpkin in her wedding dress, she looked like a rare and valuable girl
I tried hard not to wet my pants, but apart from the Lord, she was everything to me
And I vowed to be a faithful man and do all I can to make her happy.

Our honeymoon was in Bermuda and for the first evening we watched the sunset
I held her hand as we walked along the shore as our feet got soaking wet
That night was so romantic and intimate, it could've lasted forever
I kept saying to her that I will leave her never
She said it back to me, and we just slept in each other's arms
Unfortunately, after two hours, we were awakened by the alarm
The honeymoon was short, but we hoped to have a second one later in life
At that time, I was happy that I was a husband blessed with a beautiful wife
Two months later, she's pregnant and we're both filled with joy
We shopped for clothes (as we prayed for a daughter) and prepared her room full of toys
Around the 7th month into her pregnancy, she's diagnosed with full-blown AIDS
I fervently prayed she stop wasting time and get saved.

(Part 3)

As I prayed by her bedside, she decided to give her life to Christ
She finally understood that He alone is peace and His love alone will suffice
After she prayed for salvation, as the doctors and nurses stared
She bowed her head with tears in her eyes, as we listened to her prayer:

Father God in heaven,

I come to you again, Lord, just thanking you for being you. Lord, I've had a hard time; I've been through some terrible storms, but all along, you've been my Refuge; my fortress; my Rock. For a while there, Lord, I didn't realize that you were right beside me. I rejoice in knowing that you love me; that one day, I will come forth as "pure gold". Father, I know my time here on this earth is short. I've made some awful mistakes Lord and I am dealing with the consequences of those mistakes. But, I am alright now Lord because I know you are here with me, for you said in Your Word that you would never leave nor forsake me. I am so grateful to you for looking past my faults and simply meeting me at the point of my needs. What a good God you are!!! Lord, I know you had to reach way down to pick me up and I give you the glory. I regret that I didn't get to know You sooner; I regret that I didn't introduce others to You sooner so that they can have this joy that I now have. Yet, I thank you for your grace and mercy Lord; for allowing me the chance to get right with you.

Lord, I want to thank you for the godly man you sent me; I thank you for his love, his faithfulness, and his commitment to you. I know that if he does right by you, he'll do right by his family. I thank you too, Lord for this gift of life I have growing inside of me now. Lord, I don't know how long I'll have with my daughter or with my husband. In essence, I don't know what the future holds, but I thank You Lord because I know you hold the future. And because of your love for all of us, we'll be together again one day. Though I may be gone from this place, I know that you'll take care of my husband; I know that you'll bless my daughter. I pray that you continue to lead and guide my husband in the way that he should go. I pray an anointing on our daughter, that she will always know you and will always keep you first. And Lord, I couldn't ask for anything more for I know that in your hands, they will be fine.

Lord, I want to pray for my sisters out there. Sometimes Lord, we get caught up in this world system; what the world expects; what the world wants. You said in Your Word that we shouldn't conform to this world because doing so would have us follow Satan, the ruler of this world. It is not about doing things to please others, but about you and our service to you. You are all we need Lord; you are the only one, who can quench our thirst; who can make the hunger pains go away; who can dry up the tears; who can give us peace. Some of the girls I used to hang out with are coming around now and telling me how sorry they are about my condition. And while I would love to be able to be there to raise my daughter and to grow old with my husband, if it's Your will that I leave here sooner than that, it's ok because either way, all will be well with my soul. I can relate to Paul when he said "to live is Christ and to die is gain." Lord, if I could just get through to those in my past who are not saved. If only they could understand the peace I have now that I've accepted You in my heart; if they could know that regardless of what comes their way, with You, they have nothing to fear, for who can stand against God? What a good God You are, to forgive us of our sins and blot them from You mind as You give us another chance to do better. What love you have for us that you would send Your Son to die in our stead so that we may have eternal life with you. Some of the folks I used to hang with just look at me like I am crazy when I talk about you, even in my present condition. I talk about how each day we should put on our "armor" because we don't wrestle against flesh and blood, but against the spiritual forces of evil; that Satan wants us to give in to our flesh and allow our bodies to be used in a way that is not pleasing; that You said our body is a temple of the Holy Spirit; that we are not our own; that we were brought with a price. I talk about how we should be imitators of You; about how we should show our love to one another; help one another; not bring each other down; about how You will take care of our enemies if we put our trust in You; about how even though we will have trials and tribulations, You will always deliver us and bring us through. If only they would know what I know... If they would only know that as children of God, we are more than conquerors; that neither death nor life, angels nor demons, neither the present nor the future, nor any powers, neither height nor depth, nor ANYTHING else in all creation would be able to separate us from your love, through Jesus. If we put our trust in You Lord, You will see us through. You have told us that you would never let the righteous fall; that if we cast all of our cares upon You, You would handle them for us. And Lord, the only thing you can't do is fail; you are a keeper of promises. You are our creator; our all in all. And God, I thank you, that all along, your grace has been sufficient.

Lord, I pray continually for those who feel like they don't deserve anything good in life. I pray that they will come to realize that you worked it out for us to have life and to have it more abundantly. And while weeping may endure for a night, joy will surely come in the morning. You have already told us that our momentary troubles are achieving for us a far more eternal weight of glory we are looking forward to. Help us Lord, to be able to put things in perspective, that in the whole scheme of things, what we are going through is temporary, but if we hold out and hold on to You Lord, we'll have a permanent home with you one day. Lord, I look forward to the "New Jerusalem", where you will wipe every tear from our eyes, where there will be no more death, or mourning, or crying, or pain. Thank You, Lord, for saving me.

A month later, she's rushed to ICU
She's about to give birth to our daughter, a month before she's due
Andrea's placed on a respirator, and her blood pressure is high
Her heart rate was low and I couldn't speak, but only sigh
I started to pray that Christ would be glorified through her life or her death
And that she would praise Him until her final breath
After I prayed, the doctor came to me with words I dreaded everyday
Nicole Ciara Moore is born, but your wife has passed away

(Epilogue)
It's now five years after the loss of my beautiful wife
And I start to teach Nicole lessons about life

Take It from Me: Cautionary Tales from a Former Fool

She's trying hard to type this poem for me as she's sitting on my lap
And I think of Andrea when Nicole takes her naps
Andrea, I'll always see your face as I watch Nicole pursue what she's called to do
But for now, I want to say, "Andrea, Nicole and I miss you
Though we are separated now and my heart is torn apart
Know that no love can ever replace yours - my wife, Nicole's mother - you'll always live on in our hearts."

Starting Over

(This poem was inspired by Rachael Lampa's The Art).

When you give your life to Christ, it's the best move you'll ever make
Believe me you will be challenged in every step you take
Having said that, there are some issues everybody has to face
Death, temptation, your past, these are things the mind constantly retrace

Starting over is probably the hardest thing to do
Especially when catastrophe after catastrophe is constantly overtaking you
Maybe it's a lost of a loved one? Maybe it's a financial setback?
Maybe it's a love gone bad? Maybe it's a demonic attack?
Maybe you've endured a bad job? Maybe you're overcoming your past?
Maybe you think that your marriage isn't going to last?
Maybe you've hurt someone and they don't want to forgive you?
Maybe you've allowed bitterness in your life? Maybe your actions define what you do?
Maybe you feel depressed and alone? Maybe you feel you've endured so much pain?
Maybe you just feel like in your life, there's nothing to gain?
Maybe you've been abused? Maybe you've gone through a divorce?
Maybe you've been laid off? Listen, there's more that's worse
Maybe you feel like you can't go on? Maybe you're recovering from a major sin?
Maybe death is just around the bend, and you just want your life to end?
Maybe you feel like there's no way out, or there's a methodology to starting over?
Maybe you feel it's just as futile as searching for a four-leaf clover?

Listen, God loves you like no one else
But the fear of facing our biggest enemy overtakes us, looking at the self
We know God has forgiven us for the wrongs we've done
But we're trying to keep our dark secrets from the Great One
Maybe it's the fear of having to move on, maybe you feel it hurts so bad
And you feel that God won't forgive that wrong, and you cry and feel so sad
Maybe you feel your dark secret will damage your relationship with someone?
Maybe you sense that people and God won't forgive you, regardless of what you've done?
Yes, it hurts; believe me, I'm able to relate
You can't bear this burden alone; He's never too early or too late

Forgiving ourselves is hard; yes it's easier said than done
I know you realize in your mind that He's forgiven you

Pray for me as I pray for you that we cast our cares upon the Great One
Because He's waiting with open arms, don't limit Him as to what He can do

Starting over is never easy, regardless of the issue
It's OK to cry, just make sure you have some tissue
God understands your hurts, and He wants to heal your broken heart
He will give your rest, trust Him, he will never depart
Draw near to Him and He will draw near to you
That should be our desire, no matter what we say, think and do
God can still use you, remember He's the potter and we are the clay
Let Him have His rightful place, let Him have His own way.

The Arms of Love

(Sometimes we make mistakes and think that God won't forgive us. The remedy is 1 John 1:9).

How can I pray when I feel so far away?
I know I feel so bad and I can't find the words to say
How can I wrong you? Where did I go wrong?
This is my prayer, or it could be my repentance song
How can you love me when I've strayed so far?
You hate sin, because holy is what and who you are
How can I say I love you when I'm prone to sin?
Sometimes I wonder if my life will really begin
How can I praise you when my past haunts me?
Because of Your blood and your love, I'm able to see
How could you die for someone like me?
I feel so unworthy and it should've been me on a tree
How can I read your word when guilt is ever shown before me?
Because you know we're sinners and we're in need of Thee
How can you forgive me when sin is crouching at my door?
And tears pour before my face when I'm praying with my knees on the floor?
It's your forgiveness that covers me, your love that surrounds me
I want to come home; I want to be near Thee
The devil is trying to haunt and hinder my life with my past
But I also know Lord, that you're the first and the last
I want to start my life fresh and anew
So please don't take your spirit and my first love for you
Teach me your ways so I can stand strong in these days
And I can simply tell the enemy to get out of my way
I need to feel your Spirit which is truly from above
Please, Lord, wrap me in your arms of Love.

You're Still Mine
(Inspired by Hosea & Gomer)

It was a Sunday during the summer, where we accepted the Lord
We walked hand-in hand, together on one accord
God brought our hearts and spirits together
And we knew in Him this love will last forever
Time went by and I asked for your hand to wed
And I'm so thankful we held on to the principle, "no wed, no bed"
One day, during our marriage, you wanted to leave me
I cried, begged and pleaded, but you said we weren't meant to be

On that day, you packed your bags leaving no regrets
And the sweet communion we had, you wanted to forget
You found somebody else, who worshipped other lords
The enemy crept into our marriage, and broke up our three-fold cord
But deep inside my heart, you still belong to me
I don't care with the world says, God said we were meant to be
Nothing can change the fact you're still my wife
I still wear my wedding ring, and for you I'll give up my life
Even though men have turned you to other gods, I know you too well
You'll be back, and now it's time for me to rebel against the kingdom of hell
It will never prevail over you, even though right now you're trapped in deception
But I'll never give in to fear, doubt, or thoughts of rejection
I'm going to wait on the Lord for your return; I wouldn't have it any other way
And just like my love for the Lord, I love you more than words can say
Without you I have no prayer partner, I'm totally incomplete
It was predestined, and God-appointed we were to meet
Yes seasons do change, that's probably why you felt you should go
But I love you too much, and this love is real, I'll never loosen my hold!
I believe you'll return, and I'm waiting with open arms
I have faith in the God I serve, so there's no need for trusting in lucky charms
I will do what it takes to win you; I'll buy you back, if that's what it takes
I know the enemy has deceived you to think our love was a mistake.

At last you're home; it truly took some time
Now finally I'm all yours and you are all mine
You came to yourself and realized the enemy left you high and dry
The Lord heard your prayer of repentance and your cry
I'm so thankful that God sees all and knows all
He love you so much, whether you're great or little, big or small

So, as you read this, remember that Jesus loves you

He waits for you with open arms; He loves you more than I do
Don't let the enemy break your resistance down, please take heed
You're like the grass in this world, and you have to watch out for the weeds
Trouble may come for a season, but it will not last for long
And know that with the power of His might, we're strong.
Hide His word in your heart, and everything will be fine
Because He's saying to us all, "My child, you're still mine."

PART VII:
Words of Wisdom

His Unchanging Hand

(A simple poem to never let go of His unchanging hand).

I'm going to hold on, as long as it takes
I refuse to keep making the same mistake
Trying to do things on my own strength and terms
Will I ever grow out of this, will I ever learn?
His unchanging hand will see me through it all
No matter the problem, simple or complex, large or small
I'm going to hold His hand because His Hand is strong
I'm going to hold it through my battles, no matter how long
I've got my grip and I'm going to hold it tight
With all of my strength and with all of my might
This is simple, but I want you and the devil to see
That I'm standing on His Word and it's not about me
It's about my love and wanting a heart like Christ
Nothing will matter beyond that; nothing else will suffice
I refuse to be defeated; I refuse to be bound
I'm walking in His freedom, and nothing's slowing me down
My hope is on eternal things, not on this earth
It better be, especially if I've received the new birth
So, I'm going to hold His unchanging hand to the end
Because there's a better life around the bend.

It's Gonna Be Alright (My Beloved Child)
(Dedicated to Angela B Holloman)

Through trials and tribulations, storms and rain
You wonder if there will ever be an end to your pain
Through tears of frustration and tears of sorrow
You wonder if you'll ever see tomorrow
My beloved child, you're a gift from God
You're human just like us all, so don't think you're odd
Christ loves you even when no one loves you
He's a friend that can do what we can't do
You're a walking light so let it shine
He's saying I am yours and you are Mine
Rest in His care for peace shall be with you
In all of your endeavors and in all that you do
I know I'm not experiencing your kind of pain
But know that you and I together go through some torrential rain
God is allowing this to happen for a reason
So don't lose heart, for we'll know it all in due season
For our afflictions here on earth are only short-term
And will surely fade and get old like a perm
So whenever you feel hurt and your days seem dim
Tune your spirit to Psalm 121 for our help is in Him
Don't let your setbacks keep you from the prize
He loves you no matter your shape or your size
Keep a song of praise in your heart day and night
For my beloved child, don't despair, it's gonna be alright.

Seasons Change

Is your life experiencing depression or isolation?
Can you take a moment to hear this consolation?
Do you feel that life has dished you a bad blow?
You try to reason why, but it seems that you'll never know
I know the feeling; it can feel very cold
And the stronghold in your life feels like you're forced to hold
Is the bed your dwelling place where you cry your tears?
And just thinking about tomorrow increases your fears?
Remember that seasons and feelings do change
Let His love in, and let your life be rearranged
Did you forget that your help comes from the Lord?
Don't run away, His body is to be on one accord
Your dry spell won't last forever
I'll say it till you understand; He'll leave you never
Do we sing encouraging songs, and forget them when we're in trouble?
Remember Psalm 91 and that He'll be there on the double
To close this simple, short poem, your life doesn't have to be deranged
So cast your cares on Him, and remember that...
Seasons must,
Seasons will,
Seasons have,
Seasons shall,
Seasons do change!

When Your Life Is Low

Listen my friend, you are special to me
And you have been empowered to be what you're called to be
Life is interesting; it's full of valleys and peaks
There are days when you feel strong and days when you feel weak
My friend, your struggle is my struggle, and you're not alone
He walks with us everyday and wants to make His house our home
It's my prayer this will encourage you and pick you up
His love is like herbal tea, that sweet smell in your mug or cup
No matter what you're going through, His grace is sufficient for Thee
He will always be there for you, and He will always be there for me
Keep your mind stayed on Him to experience that perfect peace
Your troubles will simply fade away, and eventually have to cease
He wants His peace to surpass all of your understanding
It might seem like a challenge, and to your flesh it may seem demanding
Trust me my friend, I see and imagine the tears you cry
Let me encourage you as a brother, as we long for the sweet by and by
Our lives are like the weather, facing sunny days and rain
We love the joyful times in our lives, but we don't want to see the rain
Storms in life are to keep you in line with His love
Just call His name, and your heart will receive a kiss from above
I praise God when I see a rainbow; it shows me that He really cares
The rainbow after the storm gives me the strength to face what I alone can't bear

He wants to walk with you through the fire; He wants to be your closest friend
Open your heart to Him, and unlike man, He will hold you to the end
He's not a fair-weather friend; He's not a man that He should lie
If you surrender your all to Him, He will give you eternal rest when you die

This is a simple poem to let you know
That He will hold you like an infant when you feel your life is low
If you ever feel discouraged again, after you read this letter
Think back to when your life was low, He comforted you, and you felt better
Our life struggles won't end until we've breathed our last breath
But if we're in Him, nothing can separate that fellowship, including death
Keep His Word in your heart, so that others will know
You are genuine, and can encourage them when their dream seems to not grow
I love you my friend, and God has given you a special glow
Let it shine, because you now know who to turn to when your life is low.

Where Is Your Dream?

Where is your dream? This is your question for the day
And I pray that you don't repel the words I'm about to say
If I didn't love you, then this poem would never have came about
But we have a dream that we must fulfill before our time here on earth runs out
Please listen to me, here's where the lesson begins
I hope that you can make it till the very end

If you remember the story of Joseph and the trials he had to face
They hated him, they sold him, they wanted him removed leaving no trace
The only thing they gave to their father was a coat full of blood
In short, Joseph went through the fire, and he went through the flood
What started it all was that Joseph's dream was conceived by the Lord
Because God had a purpose, that His children could walk with Him on one accord
The brothers were being used by the enemy and they wanted to take Joseph out
And it's the same today, where the enemy is seeking and roaring about
He's looking for someone who's not totally committed to Christ
Because he knows that lip service without true repentance will not suffice

Look back at your high school days, what was the dream that God gave you?
And you knew without a doubt, that's what you were called to do?
What has become of that? What are you doing with that dream now?
Have you been a part of the rat race? Do you wonder if it's still possible somehow?
Mind you I'm talking about a dream that's right and consistent with the Word of the Lord
Because you need to know that we have got to come together on one accord
This is the time, this is your day
Hopefully this poem will give you a plan, and point you to the right and only way

You need to know that God gave you a talent, a dream, a purpose for your life
And when He gives it to you, it might come easy, but don't expect ease without strife
If you don't fulfill your dream, you're robbing God and somebody else
And with that said, your dream isn't meant for you to keep to yourself
If you remember the story about Samson, who was a godly man short of priesthood
He had a purpose, to fulfill God's will the best that he could
But he ran upon Delilah, a woman who was hired by some men

Take It from Me: Cautionary Tales from a Former Fool

They used her to get to him, and what happened then?
God's spirit was removed and the devil got his way
Maybe this is you; maybe this is your condition today
The devil is using someone that you love to get you to sin
Now here's your plan of action, so that the devil doesn't win
Understand this is a spiritual battle; the devil doesn't want you to succeed
If you keep reading Ephesians 6, you've got all that you need
You've got to say no, and get them out of your sight
It's easier to do what's convenient than to do what's right
If you don't, you'll be a casualty
And we have too many Christians, giving up their royalty

Maybe you're like Jonah, and are afraid to fulfill His call
You're running away, not wanting to have anything to do with it at all
You've faced too many challenges because of your flesh and the weight of your past
Remember your steps have been ordered, you have a purpose that will forever last
Don't run away from your current struggles, receive His Word in your heart
Give everything that you face to Him, and begin from the start

Maybe you're running with somebody just because they might be your breakthrough
God provides true breakthrough, just stay humble and let Him use you
Maybe you're allowing too many demonic spirits to have access to your heart and mind
Repel it; read Psalm 1 and 73, a treasure is what you will find
Maybe you feel like the pursuit of your dream is taking too long
Watch, stand fast in the faith; be brave and be strong

Maybe you're in a complacent state, and you feel comfortable that way
But let me say this, complacency will hurt your present and future days

Who has the dream of going home to be with Christ someday?
That better be your dream if you believe, He is definitely the only way
If this is your dream, get your house ready, in order, and renovated
Make sure that your relationship with Him is constantly cultivated
Get the weeds out of your life; I know this may be painful for some
But for your dream and His call, do it and His blessing to you will come.

Who Are Your Friends?

Take an inventory of your life, what do you see?
Who's in your life that does or doesn't need to be?
Yes, I'm talking about your friends, that's what this is all about
The person that you love the most could sell you out
Do they smile in your face? Do they want to take your place?
I'm sure you'll agree this affects you and me
I thought I knew about him; I thought she was real
But we gave into our emotions and fell for the whip appeal

As you look at your life, have you ever been hurt before?
Have you ever been lied on? Do you feel you can't take it anymore?
Did he or she steal your dream from you? Did they sell you out?
Did they cause you to quench His love? Did they cause you to scream and shout?
Have you ever been used before? Have you ever been deceived?
Have you tried to love somebody and yet they weren't ready to receive?
Have people been with you when things are going right?
But when things take a bad turn, those same people are out of sight?
They point a finger at you, and blame you for the issue
Causing you to cry yourself to sleep with your pillow as your tissue

All of these questions amount to nothing in reality
We're relying on ourselves for the answer, and not the real "G"
Continue with the inventory, you might want to make a list
Divide it in three columns so that way no one in your life will be exempt or missed
People in your life fall into one of three categories
They are a part of our lives to complete our life's story
However, the enemy will sow tares that we have to walk through
I have to walk through them, and so do you
Some friendships in our lives need to take the ax of regulation
And then there are some friendships that need the strength of cultivation
The final ax I hope doesn't stir in your heart the word "hate"
But for your salvation and walk with Christ, some need the ax labeled terminate

Please keep the love of Christ in your heart as you're doing this exercise
We're to be harmless as doves and like serpents, be very wise.
Yes, this is about your friends, because our salvation is what matters in the end
We're going to make it together; with Christ as our most faithful friend.

PART VIII:
Closing Thoughts

A Place in My Heart

(This is dedicated to my past friends, present friends and future friends).

As time goes by and memories have faded
Sometimes it might make your world seem jaded
You passed through my life for a definitive reason
It could be for a lifetime, or just a season
I treasure the fact of meeting you in this life
Just knowing you're special to my heart will suffice
There are some people I've hurt, and some that I've loved
There are some who flew away just like a dove
If I could relive some things from my past
I'd be more sensitive and make our friendship last
I'd treasure the gifts you left in my heart
Your laughter, your joy, you gave me a fresh start
But you're gone from me, maybe for a moment or for life
I wish this pain weren't as sharp as a knife
So if you hear my cry and we communicate today
I simply say that I love you, what more can I say?
Though you're distant from me, and you're no longer with me
I'll never forget you as long as I'm free
There may be some people that I will meet before I die
I'll learn from my mistakes and live life through my Father's eyes
So, wherever you go, whether near or far
Just know that you have a place in my heart.

"If I Didn't Say........."

(Sometimes we forget tomorrow is never promised).

If I didn't say I love you before, I'm saying it now
Though my expression doesn't belie it, my heart takes a bow
You are special to me; you are the only key that unlocks my heart
No matter where the road leads, my love for you won't depart
So if you're sad today, know that you are loved
Because the air that you breathe is truly a blessing from above
If your heart is heavy and you're trying to carry your load alone
Know that He is closer to you than your cell phone
If I didn't say I love you before, please forgive me
Charge it to my head, because I'm only human, you see
That I'm a sinner separated by my own sin
Pray for me as I pray for you to let forever begin
I know this is hard for someone to bear
But a bandage of God's love is needed before your heart tears
Why did you choose me to be your friend?
I don't deserve somebody like you, even if it's to be till the end
Through my mistakes and my faults, you still loved me for me
And I thank you for not hanging me on a tree
I know I'm not Christ, so let's keep this friendship together
But just know that you'll be in my heart forever
Don't worry, I'm OK, even if this poem doesn't seem so
I want you to know that you're loved no matter where you go
It's time for me to end this my friend
Whether you're near or far, I'll love you till the end.

Thank You

(I dedicate this poem to everyone in my life).

This poem was inspired by a dream from last night
I learned something, and there are some things that need to be made right
Take a moment, and reflect back to your high school years
I know for some, you'll have to fight your tears
Don't focus on the bad things, that's not what this is all about
I want you to set your mind at ease, there's no need to scream and shout
Who in your high school years made you think about a real love?
I'm talking about being in a real relationship, that's truly sent from up above
Who in your high school years brought out the best in you?
Whether it is cooking, singing, or whatever He called you to do
Who in your high school years made you think about a relationship with Christ?
Who showed you that He's the only way and no one else would suffice
Who in your high school years taught you a lesson that has blessed you now?
Good things and bad things, there's no need to hold your head down
Now take these questions, and ask who has impacted your life today?
Who has blessed you, cared about your spiritual walk, and wouldn't hurt you in any way?
There are so many people then and now that have truly blessed me
And there are some who I wished knew they've helped me fulfill my present destiny
So I say thank you for crossing my path in this walk
Thank you for your challenges, rebukes, and encouraging me to walk my talk
It's my prayer to God that He lets those who aren't reading this know
That I'm grateful to have met them and I now let my feelings show
I'll try to never miss an opportunity to count the blessings He's given me
For without His divine intervention in my life, where would I be?

Continuing on, many now and then have taught me about love
And what to look for, of course first of all it's from above
Many now and then have taught me numerous things
From patience to understanding and the need to stay under His wing
I thank you for those things and thank you for longsuffering with me
I know that I can be difficult at times, and annoying as a bee
To the elders in my life, I'm truly grateful for you
Your rebukes and challenges have propelled me and prepared me for what I'm called to do

I know I can seem stubborn and even zealous to some extent
Charge it to my head and not my heart's intent

Take It from Me: Cautionary Tales from a Former Fool

When you care about someone you really love, and know they deserve better
You want to encourage them and see they obey God's Word to the letter
I know what we may want as encouragement may not line up to His will
But sometimes we need to surrender our will and just stand still

I say thank you for allowing me to speak into your life
I say thank you for speaking right back to mine
Forgive me for causing you any pain or strife
Take this thank you as a token for the difference you made in my life

So, take a moment to say thank you to those who have blessed you
Who care about your spiritual walk and what He's called you to do
I love you so much and one day our bodies will be captured
And I long for the day when I'll see you all in the rapture.

About The Author

Tremayne Moore, founder of Maynetre Manuscripts, LLC, is an accountant, a writer, a psalmist, a griot, and a spoken word motivational speaker.

He holds a Bachelor of Science Degree in Accounting from Florida Agricultural & Mechanical University and a Bachelor of Science Degree in Management Information Systems from Florida State University.

Tremayne's life can be summarized with a quote from the Apostle Paul from Philippians: Christ shall be magnified in my body; whether by life or by death.

To write Tremayne or to contact him for speaking engagements, address Maynetre Manuscripts, LLC; Post Office Box 14823; Tallahassee, FL 32317; or email him at: tremayne_moore@yahoo.com.

www.ingramcontent.com/pod-product-compliance
Lightning Source LLC
LaVergne TN
LVHW050937080826
845145LV00004B/1308

* 9 7 8 0 6 1 5 2 9 1 7 5 8 *